1-15-2022

To Brian

Much Love

Anton Zilahi

I READ MINDS

And So Do You!

I READ MINDS

And So Do You!

Anton Josef Zellmann

Copyright © 2004 by Anton Josef Zellmann

Illustrated by Simeon Liebman

Library of Congress Number: 2003099763

ISBN: 0-9763325-0

All rights reserved. No part of this book may be reproduced, stored in a retrieval system, or transmitted by any means–electronic, mechanical, photocopying, recording or otherwise–without written permission from the author.

This book was printed in the United States of America.

To order additional copies of this book, contact:
orders@zellmannpublishing.com

Zellmann Publishing, LLC
420 Springwood Ct.
Canton, GA 30115
770 345-7266
770 345-7265 - Fax
www.zellmannpublishing.com

CONTENTS

FOREWORD xiii

ACKNOWLEDGMENTS xv

CHAPTER ONE
   Introduction: "Why Read Minds?" 1
      Memory as the Link to All Other Mental Skills 3
      Perfect Memory Abilities 6
      Memorize by Rote or by Comprehension? 8
      Am I Psychic? 9
      Conscious or Unconscious State of Mind 12
      This Book 13

CHAPTER TWO
   Mind to Mind: It's All about Communication 17
      The Sender 18
      The Communication Environment 20
      The Receiver 21
      The Communication Demons 23
      The Communication Process 24
      The First Step Is Reading Our Own Minds 25

CHAPTER THREE
   The I/You Concept: Beyond My Self-Talk 27
      Parental Messages 33
      Protecting Myself 34
      Thinking Outside My Small Box 36
      It's All about Change! 37
      Reading and Thinking in the First Person 40

CHAPTER FOUR

My Brain: The Nuts and Bolts of My Memory 43
   How My Brain Is Wired 44
   Memory and My Brain 46
   Protecting My Memory with a Healthy Brain 48
   Nutrition 48
   Aerobic Exercise 50
   Emotional State 51
   Stimulation 52

CHAPTER FIVE

NLP: A Window to My Thinking 55
   Three Kinds of Thinking Processes 57
   Learning My Own Preferred Thinking Processes 59
   Learning the Preferred Thinking Processes
   of Others 60
   Eye-Accessing Cues 63
   My Memory 65
   Concentration—Sister to Memory 71
   Rhyming Number Pegs 72
   It's All about Choice 80

CHAPTER SIX

Beliefs: I Do What I Believe I Can Do 81
   My Beliefs and My Self-Talk 81
   Caught in the Classic Vicious Belief Cycle 82
   My Positive and Negative Beliefs 83
   The Power of My Assumptions 85
   Testing Assumptions 87
   The Filter of My Beliefs and My Assumptions 93
   The Importance of My Choices 95
   My Level of Comfort and My Risk-Taking 97
   My Beliefs and My Memory 100
   My Three-Minute Exercise
   for Remembering Names 100
   Pop the Balloon! 104

AIR: Attention, Interest, and Repeat 107
Homework—Practice Makes Perfect! 109

CHAPTER SEVEN
Perception: I See What I Think I See 111
   Back to the Power of My Assumptions 112
   My Perception and Its Context 113
   Context Affects My Behavior 115
   Other Influences on My Perception 118
   Perception and My Memory: Visualization 119

CHAPTER EIGHT
Listening: I Hear What I Want to Hear 123
   Active Listening and
   the Effective Listening Pyramid 125
   The First Step in Effective Listening: I Am
   Committed to Stop Talking 127
   The Second Step in Effective Listening: I Am
   Committed to Pay Attention 128
   The Third Step in Effective Listening: I Am
   Committed to Observe Nonverbal Messages 129
   The Fourth Step in Effective Listening: I Am
   Committed to Listen Objectively 130
   The Fifth Step in Effective Listening: I Am
   Committed to Listen Analytically 131
   The Sixth Step in Effective Listening: I Am
   Committed to Listen with Empathy 132
   Practice Effective Listening 133

CHAPTER NINE
Intuition: My Other Sense 135
   But What Do I Really Propose by "Intuition"? 137
   A Real-Life Example of Conscious Intuition 138
   Lois's Perspective 139
   Anton's Perspective 142
   Intuition Works 144

Could It Be Simply Another Habit? 145
Creating a New Mind-Set 147
Overview—Honing My Intuitive Process 147
A Closer Look 148
Phase One: Prepare Physically and Mentally 149
I Relax My Body and Mind 149
I Suspend My Assumptions and Judgments 150
I Become Consciously Present 151
Phase Two: "Tapping" into My Intuition 152
I Observe and Discern My Self-Talk 152
I Ask Myself Questions and Observe
My Answers 153
I Check for Any Noticeable Results 155
I Practice, Practice, and Practice Some More 155
A $10,000 Intuitive Hit 156

CHAPTER TEN
Creativity: Expanding My Mind 161
Developing My Creativity Skill 161
My Assumptions and My Creativity 166
Framing and Creativity 171
A Note on My Brain and Creativity 175

CHAPTER ELEVEN
A Brief Pause: Recapping the Messages 177
Commitments and Benefits 177
Psychic Awareness 178
I/You Concept 178
Human Brain 179
Neuro-Linguistic Programming (NLP) 180
Beliefs and Assumptions 181
What We See 182
What We Hear 183
Intuition—My Other Sense 183
Visualize, Imagine, and Create 184

CHAPTER TWELVE

Reading My Own Mind: I Am a Living Example 187
    Motivated By Crisis 188
    Meditation and Visualization 189
    A Conscious Use of My Belief System 190
    Choice Originates from a Belief 191
    Creative Insight 191
    Drawing upon My Enhanced Mind Skills 192
    Beliefs and Assumptions 194
    I Am Always Using My Willpower: Either I Will
    or I Will Not 194
    Using Mnemonics to Organize and Recall 196
    Expectations Can Often Lead to Disappointment 197
    Perception 198
    Listening 199
    In the End, I Was Successful 199

CHAPTER THIRTEEN

Understanding and Reading Your Own Mind:
All It Takes Is Practice 201
    Rising Above Flatland 201
    Start with Self-Talk 203
        Exercise One: Study Yourself 204
        Exercise Two: Challenge Yourself 206
        Exercise Three: Expand Yourself 207
        Exercise Four: Suspend Your Judgments 209
        Exercise Five: Use Your Subliminal Mind 210
    You've Been Reading Your Mind 213

CHAPTER FOURTEEN

At Last: Reading Their Minds 215
    Exercise One: Study Them without
    Interacting 216
    Exercise Two: Study Them While You
    Interact 217

Exercise Three: Understand Their
Point of View 220
Exercise Four: Step into Their Shoes 223
You're Now Reading the Minds of Others 225

CHAPTER FIFTEEN
A Work in Progress: I Will or I Will Not 227
Have You and I Achieved
What We Set Out to Do? 227
Understanding the Facts as I Perceive Them 228
The Payoff 230
What This All Means to Me 231
I Thank All Who Have Encouraged Me 233

INDEX 235

ABOUT THE AUTHOR 243

I dedicate this book to the scores of people who were present at the thousands of presentations I delivered over the past thirty years. I especially wish to honor those who encouraged me to write this book and requested I expand on the personal stories, mind skill knowledge, and exercises I communicated to them during the brief time we shared together. I remain humbled by their interest, their questions, and their acceptance of my oftentimes unique expressions about the workings of my mind.

FOREWORD

To meet and know Anton Zellmann is a truly unique experience. He's open and completely revealing of himself. At the same time, he's the mysterious mentalist who can read your mind. He tells you he hasn't had much education, and yet when he talks, one can't help but be impressed by his wellspring of knowledge. One moment he's the extroverted salesman, and the next moment he's a concerned, empathic listener.

To read this book is like meeting Anton Zellmann. As you work your way through the many pages of wisdom, you will experience all of the facets of his fascinating personality. One moment he will be telling you very revealing personal things about himself. At another moment, he will be teasing you with illusions. At times he will be the man next door, sharing some common-sense guidelines about life. At other times he will be a professor, guiding you to some recent scientific discoveries. On some pages, he will tell you how to sell yourself, while on others he will be teaching you how to open yourself up to listening.

To read this book is to take a journey through Anton Zellmann's life. He describes himself as a work in progress, and you will experience him progressing from page to page.

You will learn far more than reading minds as you work your way through this book. You will learn something about how your brain works, about how you perceive your world, about how you communicate with other people. In *I Read Minds—And So Do You!* you will explore ways to awaken your innate creative ability. You will learn how to tap into your intuition. You will learn how to overcome restricting beliefs and expand your mind.

Anton doesn't pretend to be an academic. To the contrary—he goes through great lengths to show you his lack of academic experience. Yet, as I read his book, viewing it through my lens of traditionally structured years of formal academic training, university teaching, and consulting, I found what he offers to be as valid and useful as any textbook.

In fact, in some sense, his book is far more useful, because it is written in a style that communicates with people, regardless of educational levels. In my travels through his book, he taught me by sharing his life experiences.

I am very pleased to be one of Anton's friends. You will experience a touch of that same intimacy yourself when you read this book.

I highly recommend you turn the page and embark on Anton's journey. You, as did I, will find yourself immersed in the colorful, fascinating, and impressive world of Anton Zellmann.

Arnie Dahlke

Arnie Dahlke, Ph.D.
December 8, 2003
Los Angeles, California

ACKNOWLEDGMENTS

Before offering my sincere gratitude to those who have helped me in my first writing endeavor, I wish to clarify the spelling of my middle and last name as printed on the cover and a few pages of this book.

Will the real Anton Zellmann please stand up?

Seems like a very simple request; however, I do have an unusual story to convey about my birth name, Anton Joseph Zellmann. That's right, two *n*'s not one, and Joseph, not Josef.

Perhaps this anecdote will answer the questions of how and why that will surely crop up in the minds of those who either know me, have seen me perform, heard me speak, or simply have seen my name in print, as Anton Josef Zellman.

My mother was married five times. As a child I lived with three of her husbands. She remains married for almost forty years to her fifth husband.

My biological father, Anton Zellmann, was born in Bromberg, Germany, and my mother was born of Romanian Jewish parents in New York City. I was named Anton at birth after my father. My mother, who is now eighty-four and, well, shall I say, given to forgetfulness and has a keen talent for embellishing, tells me I was born a twin but my brother, who would have been named Joseph, was stillborn. Therefore I was given what would have been his first name Joseph as my middle name.

Shortly after my parents divorced in 1944, my mother remarried and for convenience sake I was then referred to as Joseph A. Feldman. About 1948 my mom divorced her second husband, Dave Feldman, and soon afterward married her third husband, Joseph E. McGurty. Again, for convenience sake, and because they wanted to enroll me in a Catholic school, I became known as Joseph Anthony McGurty. That name stayed with me until 1953 when I ran away from home and lived for about three years with my first stepfather, David Feldman. Once again I was known as Joseph A. Feldman. I kept this name throughout high school and into my young adult life until 1973 when, at age thirty-two, I was to attend a Bulova Watch Company sales meeting in Switzerland. This, of course, required that I apply for a passport, which in turn required a birth certificate as proof of birthplace and name.

In speaking with my mother about where exactly I was born so I could get a copy of my birth certificate, I heard for the very first time my birth name was Anton Joseph Zellmann. I ordered and received a copy of my birth certificate from the state of New York, borough of Manhattan, where I was born.

I sent the appropriate forms, a copy of my birth certificate along with a notarized letter from my mother explaining why all my credentials stated I was Joseph A. Feldman, and consequently I was able to receive a passport.

As it happened, the very next year was when I began to think about someday leaving Bulova and becoming an entertainer. To be precise, I wanted to be a magician. I had been performing small magic shows at civic and business meetings for many years.

One day I was chatting with Roy Fromer, a friend who had been involved in the magic community for many years, about how unfulfilled I felt after performing my magic show. I expressed how most often I received about twenty-five dollars' honorarium and some polite applause. I just wasn't certain why at my age I was still doing these shows and not getting any better at it.

During the conversation he said to me, "You know, Joe, you'd make a great *ESP guy*." I had no idea what he was talking about. As it turned out, Roy gave me a copy of an eight-page booklet written by the amazing and famous "thought reader," Joseph Dunninger.

I read it and my interest was piqued. So the next day, I returned to speak with Roy. During that conversation, the new

ACKNOWLEDGEMENTS

spelling of my birth name was born. Roy suggested that a person who was going to perform as a *ESP guy* needed a more dramatic-sounding name than Joe Feldman. I told him I had recently learned my birth name was Anton Joseph Zellmann. He said, "Now that's a great stage name for a guy who is going to read people's minds. But it's a bit too long, let's change the Joseph to Josef, and remove one *n* from your last name." I thought about it for a few days, contacted a lawyer, and had my name legally changed to Anton Josef Zellman.

So here I am, thirty years later, about to see my first book in print, and it just seems right to revert back to my real birth surname of Zellmann. But I think I'll hold on to the Josef for a while longer. And so I have.

With regards to the writing of this book, I wish to emphasize my everlasting appreciation to many special souls who are so very dear to me, and whose contributions have helped to make the writing of this book a joyful reality. First and foremost is my dear wife, Lois. Her unwavering love and spiritual support continues to inspire me to achieve and grow.

I want to express my eternal gratitude to my first mentor, Howard Nease, who so unselfishly guided me as well as thousands of others toward a path of consciousness and personal responsibility.

I offer my grateful indebtedness to my cherished friend and exceptional consultant, Arnie Dahlke, who labored so diligently to assist me in shaping the language and continuity of this book.

I proudly thank my two daughters, Laurie Beth Kruszynski and Patricia Ann Stanton, for skillfully editing my work during its first draft for correct grammar, spelling, and punctuation.

I lovingly acknowledge my brother-in-law, Larry Wilson, who reviewed this book in its early stages and offered me encouragement and many expert ideas about how to form my book so it would be more readable and comprehensible.

I also wish to extend my gratitude to my friend and fellow Rotarian, Jerry Thacker, who provided me with his written thoughts about many aspects of my book.

And lastly, a special thank you to my colleague and fellow performer, Robert Blumele, who demonstrated over and over again his generosity and patience as he reviewed and edited my manuscript prior to its submission for publication.

CHAPTER ONE

Introduction: "Why Read Minds?"

> Minds are like parachutes—they function best when open.
>
> —Lord Thomas Dewar (1864-1930)
> Scottish philanthropist

I Read Minds: And So Do You!

Now there is an unusual title for a book. I will bet you, like most people, immediately think I am going to teach you some magic, something out of the ordinary, something "psychic."

Not at all; in fact, I am going to do just the opposite. I am going to offer you some very practical information that will, if understood and practiced, help you learn to "read minds." *Especially your own!*

My truth is I am convinced everyone is already reading minds. Think about this. While I am in conversation with someone, am I not using my mind to understand (read) his or her mind? When I think and search my memory for an answer, a solution, a fact, or use my creative abilities to design a new idea, am I not truly reading my own mind?

Are not the persons to whom I am communicating also reading their own minds as they look for connections to my communication? I think the answer to all of these questions is *yes*!

The words, the gestures, and even the movements of my eyes are communicating a thought from my mind to the mind of the viewer or listener. Of course, as a people, we have agreed that certain sounds, gestures, and facial expressions have specific meanings. But the question still remains. From where are my thoughts emanating? Are they not produced in the area of my brain that has been labeled as my mind? And where are my thoughts and communications being received? I would say they are being received in the mind of the person(s) to whom I am communicating.

Of course I realize I am proffering a unique and indeed an unusual point of view of mind reading. I also realize when people think of mind reading they are talking about knowing the most secret thoughts of someone else. To know exactly what they are thinking. Perhaps even word for word.

Well, I suspect I would have to be a very special soul to be able to consistently and accurately read the minds of others. However, being able to read my own mind is a challenge worthy of my time and effort. I am certain I can accomplish this fascinating goal. And that is what this book is all about.

Over the past twenty years I've taught hundreds of thousands of people how to improve their memory habits. Although I have been speaking to audiences about a wide variety of mind skills, I have become especially known as a memory expert.

However, what I have really been doing is showing them how to use their memory abilities to increase their understanding of themselves, to communicate more effectively with one another, and to become more successful at whatever profession they pursue, whether it's marketing, doctoring, management, or selling.

I am clear that helping people to improve their memory abilities is a simple and straightforward way to encourage them to also open up to the possibility of enhancing additional mental skills. If you have seen one of my more than five thousand memory presentations, you know that after I demonstrate what I call "perfect memory," I teach you how to accomplish exactly what you saw me do.

I take great pleasure as I witness the smiles of joy on your faces as you experience instant success. I see the excitement of accomplishment in your eyes. You begin to understand that while learning to improve your ability of memory and recall you can also achieve tremendous improvement in your ability to concentrate, to experience more accurate perceptions, to communicate more effectively, and to produce better choices and decisions.

I know this because so many of you have talked with me after my presentations. You tell me what you have learned from listening to and interacting with me at other meetings. Some tell me how they applied what I taught them and how good they feel about the success of those experiences. Others tell me how they taught my systems to their children and how it helped them achieve higher scores on their exams. They tell me that what I taught them opened them up to life skills far beyond improving their memories—to self-discovery and to greater personal and professional success.

For more than twenty years, many of you have asked me: "Do you have a book?" "No, but I'm thinking about it," I would answer. I thought to myself, "I really should do that one day."

However, I kept putting it off. All for what I thought were good reasons. I was too busy making a living. I didn't have the time. I needed more time to gather and understand my information, or maybe, the truth is I didn't know if I could do it—after all, I barely graduated from high school.

But then, one day I decided to change the way I was viewing this project. After all, I suggest to others that they are limited only by what they choose to believe about themselves and what they think they can accomplish in their lives. It was time to follow my own advice.

So here it is.

I offer my book to you as a tool to help you learn more about yourself so you can become more successful at whatever you choose to do.

Memory as the Link to All Other Mental Skills

I offer you a collection of techniques for improving your memory as a catalyst for enhancing your mental skills—concentration, creativity, intuition, and sharper and more objective thinking. In turn, these enhanced skills will free you from old mental scripts and programming, will point you along the path to self-discovery, and lead you to achieve greater personal and professional success.

My reasoning is simple. I believe my self-esteem, my self-concept, my self-confidence, how I perceive, how I communicate, how I concentrate, how I visualize, how I use my imagination, and even how I think are all directly connected to and dependent on my memory. My memory is truly a door to my inner self. I have designed this book to help you and me unlock, open, and move through that door.

Those who have learned the basic techniques by attending my sessions can use this book to learn even more. Those who have not yet seen or listened to my presentations will find I am helping you to open doors to improved self-esteem and to making more conscious and accurate choices.

You see I have really written this book for us. I am, and always will be, "a work in progress." I believe that is also true of you, the reader. As I began to write this book I asked myself why I wanted to do it. I came up with several reasons (listed as they came to mind, but not necessarily in this order). First, people are interested in knowing more about me and how I've developed into the character they see onstage, and they want to hear more about the concepts of mind about which I speak; second, I like the attention it will bring to me; third, I love to share knowledge; and fourth, I truly want to know more about myself, why I think as I do. I want to learn and to continue growing. Writing this book has, in a sense, forced me to align many different thoughts, theories, and concepts I have been reading and learning about over these past thirty years.

I first became interested in the workings of my memory when I came to the realization that all of my life I had been stuck with the notion that I could not remember information, especially for taking tests in school. I also grew up having trouble remembering people's names. In fact, even though I have always believed I have a keen mind and have always been a fast thinker, I chose not to go to college. Now I'm not suggesting I'm proud of that choice, but it is a part of my history.

When I look back, I see the single most important reason for choosing not to attend college was that I did not do well on

Introduction: "Why Read Minds?"

exams. I had difficulty absorbing and remembering information, and I didn't feel at all confident about what I did recall.

For many years I thought my problem with not passing exams was mostly due to the lack of time I had to study because I had a rather unusual schedule for a teenager.

I left my stepparents' home and began living on my own when I was fifteen years old. I'm certain my early learning years in parochial school (Saint Anthony of Padua in Greenpoint, Brooklyn) gave me the discipline to stay in school even though I had no adult supervision.

During my last two years of high school I lived at the YMCA in Knoxville, Tennessee, and was enrolled in a program called DE (Distributive Education). The program was designed to allow students to leave school early each day to gain experience in the workplace. I attended Young High School from 8:00 a.m. until 11:00 a.m. at which time I would take a bus downtown to open up the local Bijou movie theatre, where I was the manager. I closed the theatre about 11:00 p.m. and headed back to my room at the Y. With such a schedule, I really did not devote much time to study.

I guess it would be fair to say that I was a bit distracted. In addition to my full-time job managing the Bijou theatre, I had to deal with being the only kid in school who had a Jewish name, Joey Feldman. As I mentioned on the acknowledgment page of this book, Joseph was my middle name at birth, and Feldman was my first stepfather's last name. Keep in mind this was the early fifties, and kids' tolerance for a Jewish kid with a Brooklyn accent and the chutzpah to perform as the MC of a live, weekly, Saturday-morning teen show on the stage of the two-thousand-seat Tennessee Theatre didn't help matters. The truth was I couldn't wait to be done with the hostility and the rejection from many of my schoolmates. I really did wing it through those last couple of years of school.

Now that I've had time to reflect and learn, I've come to understand my poor study habits stemmed not only from being so distracted, but also because I had poor habits of concentration and memory. I just did not know how to learn. I did not know how to read well. Oh, I knew how to read words and sentences, but I had no concept of how to comprehend and retain what I was reading.

Looking back today, I realize how my newly learned skills at memory have helped to change my entire life.

Perfect Memory Abilities

An important understanding I now have about memory ability is that, barring ill health at birth, I am born into this world with good, if not perfect, memory capabilities. In fact, again assuming good health in my brain, when I leave the planet I will still have the capacity for perfect memory ability. I'm convinced it is possible to memorize and recall any amount of information we choose, and to do it at will and at any time in our lives. However, it takes a lot more than merely learning a few mnemonic (a method for memorizing) techniques. Be sure that I will make every effort to reveal throughout this book the necessary steps to accomplish this simple, yet seemingly difficult feat.

I'm also convinced that many of my problems with how I used my memory stemmed from how I was taught to memorize, or should I say *not* taught to memorize.

In my early years of schooling I never participated in a class designed specifically to teach me how my mental capacity for memory worked or how to use my ability to memorize and to access information.

I was in my mid-thirties before I attended a training session teaching me how to effectively use my powers of concentration, visualization, and imagination, all of which are important to the active process of memory and recall.

No teacher ever taught me any exercises about how to focus, about the skills of how to listen, or for that matter, how to think. Did any of your teachers ever spend class time teaching you specifically how your mind works, how you process

Introduction: "Why Read Minds?"

thought, or what role your emotions play in the processing of thoughts that lead to your actions? Probably not.

Well, I've asked these same questions of tens of thousands of people from all walks of life, and the overwhelming majority, I'd say in the range of 95 percent, answered *no* to each and every one of those questions.

Isn't that astounding? I find it truly amazing that from the earliest grades on, we are told to listen, to concentrate, to memorize, to be creative, to study, and to think.

Yet there apparently are no subjects, at least in the early grades, structured specifically to teach us *how* to increase and improve these fundamental functions of our minds.

I recently asked my daughter Laurie, who is a dedicated elementary school teacher and who currently works in her district in staff development, if my statement still holds true today. She told me today's curriculum does allow for teaching some of these skills. For example, students learn comprehension strategies such as use of prior knowledge, inferring, summarizing, imaging, clarifying, and monitoring. When used, these strategies allow the student to think about his/her own thinking process, which is known as metacognition.

However, she explains that these strategies are usually taught within the context of reading, language arts, and the sciences rather than as specific subjects called memory, concentration, listening, or perception.

As I understand it, the big difference in today's methods of teaching is that the use of rote memorization is balanced with strategies that also teach comprehension.

What I do recall is that I was instructed, although without explanation, to use the rote system to force information into my brain, so at some future date I could spit it out, word for word, to participate in a class project or to pass an exam.

The rote system does work. After all, we do learn the alphabet, how to add and subtract, the multiplication tables, and eventually how to read, write, and spell through the process of repetition. But look at how long it takes and how tedious it is to learn with this old-fashioned method.

Mnemonics was not taught in the school systems I attended, and so I continued to use the rote system of memorizing throughout my schooling. When studying for an exam I would read and repeat specific words or numbers aloud over and over again until I felt I had them in their correct order. It was the only method I knew.

Today I understand that what I was doing is commonly referred to as cramming. Given my time restrictions, it seemed as though I was always cramming. It's not what learning should be about.

In fact, my dictionary defines "cramming" as preparing for an examination in a hurried, intensive way. The operative word here is "intensive," which can be defined as strained and filled with action or emotion. For me the action was procrastination, and the emotions were anxiety and fear.

When using the rote system of memorizing, if I happened to forget one or two words, or place them in the wrong order, I was apt to go into a trance with worry. Then factor in having to complete the test in a specific amount of time, and I just found it too difficult to recall any part of the information at all.

Memorize by Rote or by Comprehension?

Research indicates that I can learn mechanically by rote, or I can learn by understanding. Mechanical learning is good for remembering simple tasks, but it does have its drawbacks. Rote memorization, especially of something that has no significance or meaning to me, will not be retained by my memory, at least not as long as information I truly understand.

Introduction: "Why Read Minds?"

If I want to remember something for a long time, then it pays to first comprehend it.

Another point to consider is that memory in everyday life is rarely based on rote retention of detail. Instead, it relies heavily on remembering meaning, for example, the meaning of a passage, the meaning of a conversation, or the meaning of an event.

If I'm absolutely certain surface knowledge is enough, I really don't want to know the information, I just want to remember it; then I can rely on simple mnemonic techniques.

Sometimes using both methods pays off. My recommendation when studying for exams or a speech is to first read the material for enjoyment, for interest, and for comprehension. Mark any information you may want to store away with a highlighter. Then go back over the material and use the memory system I will describe in chapter 5 to store away those points you want to access from your memory banks at some later date.

By the way, the memory techniques I will be describing have been available to us for several thousand years. I don't claim authorship for them. In fact, almost every good book or recording about mnemonic techniques will describe basically the same methods.

Naturally, all authors or speakers bring to their discussions their own style of composition and personal charisma. Hopefully I have added a few twists and turns that you may find new and refreshing.

Am I Psychic?

Now, just before I begin to offer you insights as to the tools required to "read minds," I want to clear up what I see as a common misunderstanding about the term "psychic."

I recently asked an audience, "How many psychics do I have in this room? Please raise your hand if you are psychic."

One woman raised her hand.

"Just one?" I noted. "Well, that's very interesting—we have approximately one hundred fifty people in this room and only one person raised her hand."

It was no surprise to me. It happens every time I ask an audience that question. I've come to the conclusion over the years that people don't raise their hands because they're not really confident about what it is to be psychic nor do they want to be thought of as "flaky" or as a "kook."

So I pushed my audience further. I pointed to people and asked, "What does it mean to you to be psychic?" Here are some of their responses.

"I think it is having some insights into things that are not obvious or apparent."

"To know something before it is going to happen."

"Unspoken communication, to read minds, to project and receive thoughts."

"To find lost objects—to locate and then move or bend objects with the mind."

These are virtually always the kinds of statements I hear when I ask people to tell me what they think it means to be psychic. There is often a connotation of charlatan, fake, and on occasion, a notion of entertainment running through it all.

In fact, we have become so accustomed to discounting the word "psychic" we have disassociated ourselves from being psychic. It's time for me to spell out what the word "psychic" really means.

Over the years I have looked up the word "psychic" in a variety of dictionaries, and they all provide about the same definition. The word "psychic" comes from the Greek word "psyche," and its primary meaning is "of the soul, of the mind." It doesn't say anything about being weird, occult, crazy, or foolish. It doesn't say reading minds, looking into the future, or bending spoons. It simply says "of the mind." It makes a distinction between physical and mental. We human beings are grounded in both our physical and mental worlds.

So, not only are we physical, we are also mental—we are all psychics.

You and I, every day of our lives, are using our psychic awareness, although most of us are doing it unconsciously. My memory, for example, is a psychic function of my mind that I exercise each and every day of my life. My memory is a psychic awareness a mental ability, that amazing ability to be able to store away information and access it at will. Think about it. When I remember something, *I am automatically reading my own mind.*

Some dictionaries also add the language "beyond known physical processes."

Well, aren't my functions of memory, concentration, imagination, and even thought, beyond a physical process? Aren't they, instead, all a process of my mind?

Oh, of course there are chemical and electrical processes taking place in my brain and body, and they are made up of physical matter. I will address this in some detail in chapter 4. But what about my mind? Once all the chemical reactions and interactions take place and all of the necessary electrical impulses occur, isn't the result of all of that mental, rather than physical? Couldn't my mind be considered as being beyond physical processes?

Imagine with me, if you will, that the best way to tap into more of my mind's potential may be as simple as making better use of those faculties of mind I already have working for me. For instance, my ability to store and quickly access information.

Now, what does this tell me? It tells me that the first step to take if I want to learn to read the minds of others is to fully understand how to read my own mind and how it works.

I am not going to suggest that to be an easy task, but it can be accomplished. And that's what this book is all about.

Conscious or Unconscious State of Mind

I want to be perfectly clear about a few things from the start. I am not suggesting that I know everything about my own mind, let alone yours. However, I have collected a ton of information about mind skills over the years, some of which I have reality tested.

Although I've just attained my sixty-third birthday, I must admit to becoming only somewhat conscious about twenty-seven years ago, when I began my personal journey towards understanding my own mind. It came as a huge surprise to me to learn I was totally responsible for my thoughts and the consequences of those thoughts.

Quite frankly, I've spent a good portion of my life in an unconscious state of mind. By that I mean I allowed my life to be guided mostly by my emotions, by how I felt about this or that. I had no concept of the fact that I was in charge of my thinking and the results of my thinking. I assumed that whatever came my way was that with which I had to deal. Whatever hand life dealt to me was the hand I had to play, and I therefore felt justified in complaining about it rather than doing something about it.

Oh, I knew how to finagle (manipulate) and persuade others to give me what I wanted. But the notion that I could mold my own thoughts and control my emotions never occurred to me— that is, until I came to a point in my life where I was about to lose all I had—my family, my job, my health, and perhaps even my mind. I know that sounds a bit dramatic, but that's the way it seemed to me at the time.

So, what changed? What magic formula did I discover? What turned my life around? In the midst of being an emotional wreck, I was fortunate to meet my wife, Lois. Through Lois and her circle of friends and acquaintances, I discovered another world where people were willing to shed their lifelong baggage and take charge of their lives—to think and behave in ways that produced positive results.

INTRODUCTION: "WHY READ MINDS?"

By the way, the story of how Lois and I met is a perfect personal example of a true "psychic" experience. It's really a terrific story, and I do intend to tell it in another chapter.

It is my intent to make a huge impression on you from the start so you will look forward to reading every page of this book. Most importantly, I really do want to provide you with valuable information and interesting ways to challenge your thinking, beliefs, and perceptions. Hopefully this will lead you to insights about your own thinking, how you may enhance all aspects of your mind, and—who knows—perhaps how to consciously read the minds of others.

This Book

The best way for me to share with you what I know is to first offer you a few basic tools. Once you've mastered those you can really roll up your sleeves and get to work.

In chapter 2, "Mind to Mind: It's All about Communication," I will provide you with an overall framework for thinking about the tools as you learn them. Reading minds is really a form of communication. And the communication process is more complex than most people realize. In this chapter, I will describe the many facets of communication—the many elements that influence both my ability to communicate to other people and my ability to comprehend what they are communicating to me.

Given this framework, I will set the stage for mastering those tools in chapter 3, "The I/You Concept: Beyond My Self-Talk," by introducing to you a concept I've been thinking about and working with for twenty-five years. It is a different way to look at myself and at my relationships with people and the world around me. It is a mental set that has changed my thinking and thus my life. I believe what I call the I/You Concept will set the stage for your total absorption of the positive messages you'll learn as you read this book.

Then, beginning with chapter 4, "My Brain: The Nuts and Bolts of My Memory," I will talk about the physical mechanics of memory—the nuts and bolts of memory in my brain and about the care and feeding of my brain.

In chapter 5, "NLP: A Window to My Thinking," I will take you on a brief tour of Neuro-Linguistic Programming, more commonly known as NLP. This topic may sound like a mouthful, but don't be scared away. NLP gives me some simple-to-use techniques to help me do what I told you I would do for you in the beginning: show you how to read minds, beginning with your own.

Next, in chapter 6, "I Do What I Believe I Can Do," I will reveal to you my thoughts about the power of beliefs. What I believe, what I assume about people and the world around me, and how I talk to myself in my mind are all powerful determinants of what I do in life.

From there, in chapter 7, "Perception: I See What I Think I See," I will move to some thoughts about perception. My beliefs are connected to how I perceive the world. How I perceive the world is critical to how I decide to move about within it.

And then, in chapter 8, "Listening: I Hear What I Want to Hear," I will talk about another form of perception: listening. This topic brings me full circle back to memory. It is impossible for me to remember something if I do not know how to listen! I will describe several simple techniques I have used to improve my ability to listen.

In chapter 9, "Intuition: My Other Sense," I will discuss still another form of perception: intuition. Intuition helps me make sense of all of the information I absorb every day through all of my other perceptions. At any given moment, I see, hear, feel, taste, and smell much more than I realize. I use my intuition to make quick meaning of it all.

Next, in chapter 10, "Creativity: Expanding My Mind," I will describe how I use the tools I discussed in all of the previous chapters to expand my mind, to develop my creative skills, and how my beliefs, assumptions, and my "framing" of the way I see things influence my ability to create.

Introduction: "Why Read Minds?"

In chapter 11, "A Brief Pause: Recapping the Messages," I will provide a recap—a lineup of the major components to acquiring the ability to read my mind.

In chapter 12, "Reading My Own Mind: I Am a Living Example," I will discuss events in my life that clearly illustrate how I learned to apply all of the principles and concepts I've been talking about in this book at important periods in my life.

Then, in chapter 13, "Understanding and Reading Your Own Mind: All It Takes Is Practice," I will provide you with some exercises that will enable you to read your own mind. Remember what I said in the beginning of this book: the more I know and understand my own mind, the more skilled I can become at reading the minds of others.

In chapter 14, "At Last: Reading Their Minds," you will see how being able to read your own mind will enable you to read the minds of others.

Finally, in chapter 15, "A Work in Progress: I Will or I Will Not," I will conclude this work with some of my thoughts and what I learned during the time I wrote this book. I have much to learn about myself, much to accomplish; thus, I also view this book of mine as a work in progress. Even while I am crafting each page, from the first to the last, I am forever both teacher and student. I desire to convey that dynamic view to you. I want you to know yourself and your thoughts as a beautiful and continually growing work in progress.

As you read through this book, you will see that I have made every attempt to keep it lively, interesting, and filled with insightful exercises to help you nail down what you learn.

My goal is to make this book useful to you, to make it a practical guide for improving your personal and professional skills.

I must admit my present-day thinking and the topics I speak about have been shaped by an expansive variety of books, tapes, seminars, lectures, and personal experiences. The material covered in this book has been compiled from the notes, videos, memories, audio recordings, and written scripts of the thousands of presentations I have written and delivered over these wonderful and challenging years.

I am confident that if you, the reader, immerse yourself in reading every one of the following pages, perform and practice the exercises as outlined, and absorb the valuable knowledge that awaits you on every page, you will end up a different person. And you will immediately know how to put it to work to help you achieve success at whatever you choose to accomplish.

I have one important request before we begin. I'd like you to seriously consider making up your mind, right now, *to participate in every exercise in this book.* I know firsthand how easy it is to gloss over an exercise, make a judgment about it, and to mentally decide not to do the exercise. It's so easy to think, "it would take too much time," "I'm too tired," or "I already know the solution to that problem," and then move on to the next paragraph of text. You will gain so much more by fully participating.

Keep in mind your primary reason for reading this book in the first place. Hopefully, it's because you choose to commit to learning a variety of concepts and techniques that synergistically will help you to improve your memory and to read the most important mind of all—*your own!* For how can I ever expect to see into the minds of others if I cannot first understand the workings and consciously execute the powers of my own mind?

My personal wish is that the information and exercises in this book will bring to you a bit of wisdom, some laughter and joy, and perhaps a few insights as well.

So please read on and explore with me the wondrous realm of the most powerful and infinite storage system in the universe—our minds. Sit back, relax, read, learn, and please be willing to practice, practice, practice!

CHAPTER TWO

Mind to Mind: It's All about Communication

> We pass the word around; we ponder how the case is put by different people; we read the poetry; we meditate over the literature; we play the music; we change our minds; we reach an understanding. Society evolves this way, not by shouting each other down, but by the unique capacity of unique, individual human beings to comprehend each other.
>
> —Lewis Thomas (1913-1993)
> Author and physician

As you learn the tools and techniques I use to read minds and you practice the exercises I have included in this book, you will discover that, fundamentally, reading minds is communication. So it will be helpful for me to provide you with an overview of the communication process as a framework for integrating the tools you are about to learn.

Communication is something most of us take for granted. It seems that we've always known how to talk and we've always known how to listen. We can't remember a time when we were not able to do either. It seems so simple. That's why we take it for granted.

But it's not as simple as it may appear. Communication is actually an incredibly complicated process that includes a *sender*, a *receiver*, and a *communication environment*.

Here's where it gets complicated. Both the *sender* (the person sending out the communication) and the *receiver* (the person listening to the communication) have his or her own personal physical and psychological history. The *communication environment*, the setting in which the communication is taking place, includes a variety of distorting, limiting, and distracting influences.

A sender transmits a message to a receiver in a particular environment. That message gets influenced by a host of factors from the time it starts out from the sender's brain to the time it is processed in the receiver's brain. At every point along the way, the message picks up a variety of *charges* (positive or negative meanings) that affect the way the message is received and interpreted by the receiver.

Let's see how this all works.

The Sender

Suppose you and I are having a conversation. I have something I want you to hear. I start with an image or an idea in my mind.

 My first challenge is converting that idea into a verbal message so I can send it to you. I do this by "encoding" it into some symbols called "words," which I have learned over the course of my life.

Here is where the "charges" enter the process. Each word I choose picks up a charge from three places: my *personal history*, the *intent* I have in communicating my idea, and *internal factors*.

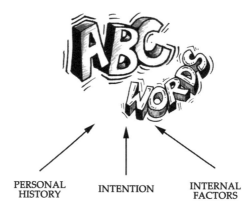

As I am exposed to and use words throughout my *personal history*, they pick up various shades of meaning, according to what is happening when I use them. Some have become charged with negative meaning, others have become charged with positive meaning, and still others have remained neutral. It's easy to see that my message to you is being influenced even before it begins!

My selection of words is further influenced by my *intent*. Why did I decide to say something to you? No matter how quickly I choose words for sending an image or an idea, most of those words are carefully selected according to my reason—my motivation—for saying them to you. Maybe I am trying to force you to do something, so I choose threatening phrases. Or maybe I am trying to please you, so I choose sentences designed to make you feel good. Perhaps I simply want to convey information to you, so I choose words I believe will most objectively do that. My *intent* is a subtle but powerful influence on my communication.

To make it even more complicated, I may not even be fully aware of the *why* behind what I am saying. For example, I could be feeling defensive and not even realize I am "stacking the deck" with negative charges.

Finally, *internal factors* influence the charges of the words I use. I may be overtired or hungry. I may be worried and tense. Maybe I just had an angry conversation with someone else, and I'm still fuming. Perhaps I am angry with you or angry with myself. Or maybe I feel dumb compared to you.

Now I've selected my words, and I am ready to communicate them to you. Once again, my *personal history*, my *intent*, and *internal factors* enter the picture, influencing the way I send my communication to you.

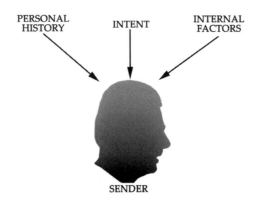

Selecting words is not the only way I communicate. My whole body gets into the act. The charges accompanying my message stimulate me to send *nonverbal* messages.

Over the years of my *personal history*, I've developed my own communication styles in a variety of situations. I may speak loudly or softly, I may or may not have eye contact with you, I may enunciate clearly or I may mumble, and so on.

Also, my *intent* in communicating with you influences how I *deliver* my message. Without even being aware of it, I may frown, I may smile, or I may scowl at you. I may hold my body in a tight stance. I may speak to you in a whining or sarcastic tone of voice.

And *internal factors* also influence how I send my message to you. I will probably have less patience when I am tired or stressed or if my intent is to defend myself against you, which will particularly affect my tone of voice, body posture, etc.

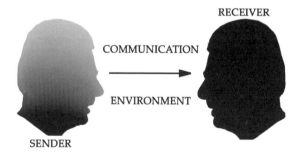

These nonverbal transmissions are automatic. They are reflexes we learn—maybe even before we learn to speak. Most of the time, we do not even know we are exhibiting them.

The Communication Environment

As I send you a message, another source of influence shapes my communication—our *communication environment.*

It may be too hot in the room. Maybe other people around us are making a lot of disturbing noise. Perhaps you are wearing what I perceive to be an ugly shirt that distracts me. Maybe you are looking around at other people as we talk. You may simply look at your watch. Or you could have a frown on your face, or a scowl, or a smile. And so on.

The way you perceive our *communication environment* further alters how *you* "process" my message. While noises may disturb me, they may not influence you at all because you were raised with five brothers and three sisters. As a native of New Mexico, a hot day might not bother me at all, but as a recent emigrant from Minnesota, that same hot day may put you in a very negative mood.

The Receiver

Now we get even more complicated. Just as my message picked up numerous charges as I formed and delivered it to you, you add charges as you receive and interpret it. You receive my words and nonverbal actions with all of their accumulated charges. You then magnify, minimize, or even change those charges, depending on what's going on inside of you and what you see going on around you.

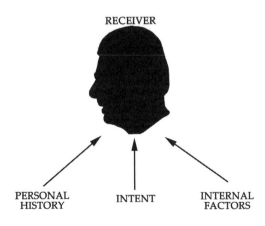

The same similar sources influence the way you receive my message—your *personal history*, your perception of my *intent*, and your *internal factors*.

Your *personal history* with the way I deliver my message will influence how you hear it. For example, I may speak with a sarcastic tone of voice. You may be comfortable with sarcasm because it was the most popular style of humor in your household as you were growing up. My sarcasm therefore does not bother you. On the other hand, if an angry parent used sarcasm frequently during your childhood, my use of it might threaten you.

Your perception of my *intent* in communicating with you adds more charges to the mixture. Are you listening to me cautiously because you think I am not trustworthy? Do you think I am trying to take advantage of you? Are you becoming defensive because you believe I have set out to attack you?

As you receive my message, *internal factors* will influence you. What you are currently thinking and feeling or how you perceive what is happening around us will affect the way you "filter" what I say. These may alter the charges on my message. Maybe you would like to be somewhere else and you feel impatient. Anything I have to say picks up a negative charge. Maybe you are hungry, you have a hard time paying attention to me, and you actually miss a charge I deliberately aimed at you!

As you receive my message, your brain begins the work of interpreting what I am communicating.

That interpretation is again influenced by the same three sources—your *personal history*, your *intent*, and *internal factors*.

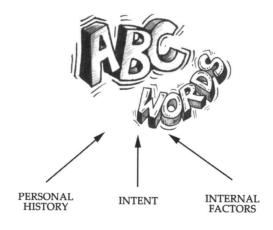

PERSONAL HISTORY   INTENT   INTERNAL FACTORS

You have your own *personal history* with the words you hear me saying. As you've used those words over the years, they have picked up various shades of meaning according to what is happening when you used them. Like me, some are now charged with negative meaning, others with positive meaning, and still others are neutral. Those charges may be the same as they are for me, or—and this is where it gets to be a problem—different from me. So the meaning I am trying to convey to you by my selecting particular words may end up meaning something entirely different to you!

We may know the same words—we may have the same words in our vocabulary. But, because of our individual personal histories, they may differ in the shades of meaning they have for each of us.

I might say, "That was a silly thing to do," and the word "silly" might mean funny to me but not to you. You might think I was accusing you of being foolish or stupid because somewhere along the way you learned to attach such a meaning to it.

Your motivational state now enters the picture—your *intent*. Why are you receiving my message? Are you listening to me because you want something from me? Are you listening to me in order to compete with me? Are you out to show me you are better than me? And so on.

In addition, your *internal factors* come into play. You may be very tired and just not thinking as clearly as usual. You may be very worried and preoccupied, which has the effect of narrowing your perceptions and thus your interpretations of what I am communicating. You may be very angry with me and actually looking for ways you can attach negative charges to my message!

The Communication Demons

Thus, by the time you have decoded my message, not only has it suffered from all of the charges it accrued while I was sending it to you, it also has been changed and burdened by the charges you added while you were receiving it.

I start with an idea or image. I choose words (often without even realizing I am choosing) to communicate my idea or image to you. My choices and the words themselves and the way I deliver them are charged by three factors—my personal history, my intentions in sending a message, and a host of other physical and psychological factors internal to me.

When I finally send the message to you, in addition to whatever is happening in our environment, you "decode" my message, influenced by the same set of three factors.

It is apparent even the simplest act of communicating to another person is very complex! And just think, all of what I just described takes place in only a few seconds.

The Communication Process

With so many elements in such a complex process—for even a single exchange between us—it is amazing we are ever able to communicate anything clearly to each other! It is also no wonder we often experience such feelings as confusion, tension, misunderstanding, discomfort, and conflict when we communicate with others.

It is apparent in looking back at the diagram on page 22 that the various negative charges involved in a transaction are the *real* demons behind the communication problems we have with each other. When I send you a message loaded with negative charges, or you perceive my message to be loaded with negative charges, I am, in effect, launching a missile at you. Your natural impulse will be to defend against it.

Some people defend by withdrawing within themselves, becoming quiet, even sullen. Others defend by attacking, by becoming belligerent, even hostile. Still others "leave the picture" by simply not listening or even actively ignoring someone talking. No matter which alternative action is taken by the receiver, it then influences the sender's next message.

The First Step Is Reading Our Own Minds

For me to engage in added successful communications, I must rid myself of—or at the very least control—my communication demons. I can only do that by learning where they come from. This means getting to know myself better, learning to understand and read my own mind. Knowing myself better will help me become more aware of the charges I add to my messages.

The more I am aware of those charges, the more power I will have to control them.

Keep this overview of the communication process in mind as you read through the rest of this book. It is a convenient framework for organizing the various tips, techniques, and exercises I share with you as I show you how to read minds—both your own and the minds of others.

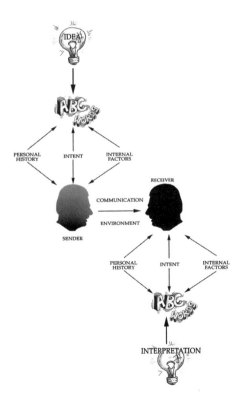

CHAPTER THREE

The I/You Concept: Beyond My Self-Talk

> The words I choose to speak, internally and externally, both to myself and to others, reinforce and fashion my life's scripts. Whatever I think about most, I am likely to manifest.
> —*Anton Josef Zellmann (b. 1941)*
> *Edutainer, speaker, author*

I strongly believe that one of the really magical qualities of my mind is I write my own life's scripts. I am the one who makes my choices for me. I bring to myself those things, those people, and those circumstances and experiences I focus on and think about the most. My choices shape my experiences.

Throughout this book, I will emphasize this concept of choice. And behind every choice—behind the scenes, so to speak—is my ongoing self-talk. The language I use to talk to myself when I think—my self-talk—is at the heart of it all.

A great number of ancient masters of thought and more modern-day motivators have, in their own way, spoken of self-talk.

King Solomon said, "What he thinketh in his heart, so is he."

William James wrote, "Whatever the mind of man can conceive and believe, it can achieve."

Napoleon Hill suggested, "We are the sum total of our most prominent and dominant thoughts."

A more modern-day motivator and a salesman's salesman, Zig Ziglar, claims, "If your business is sinking, your thinking is stinking." I believe self-talk is one of the most powerful functions of my mind. I place it right up there with visualization and imagination. It is a magical tool, and I must use it wisely.

I don't think my mind has a sense of humor. It does not decipher reality from actuality. It simply senses and reacts to commands that are triggered by my biochemistry, my stimulated neurons, and equally as important, by my moods and my thoughts.

This brings me to my I/You Concept. This perception or concept became apparent to me about twenty-five years ago. It came to me as one of those rare "aha" experiences.

At the time, I was living in Toledo, Ohio, and two significant events occurred.

The first was a comment made to me by Howard Nease, the owner and master trainer of Personal Dynamics, Inc. Howard was facilitating the first personal growth seminar I had ever attended. As I mentioned in the preface, Howard, in one sense, was my mentor, because he was the first teacher on my newly discovered path to becoming a responsible and conscious, thinking person. As I recall the incident, I was telling Howard and the other students in this weeklong training about an episode in my life. I said something like "You know, when we have something like that happen to us we—"

Howard quickly interrupted me and calmly asked, "What's this 'we'? Do you have a mouse in your pocket? Tell us what happened to you. You can't speak for everyone in this room. It's your experience, not theirs." I immediately caught on and rephrased my statement to: "When I have something like that happen to me, I—"

At the time it seemed like a sensible thing to do. But I didn't give it any more thought until about a year later when the second

The I/You Concept: Beyond My Self-Talk

event occured that caused me to conceive of the I/You Concept. I was attending a luncheon meeting of The Optimist Club of which I was an active member.

The Optimist Club is an international civic organization with lofty, yet attainable, goals: be optimistic about all outcomes in any situation and be of help to the community; particularly be of help to children.

My local chapter of the club met once a month to share fellowship and to plan the activities we would undertake to accomplish our goals in the community.

One of the rituals at each meeting was to stand up at the end of the meeting and to collectively recite aloud the Optimist Creed, which was authored in 1912 by Christian D. Larson, an advocate of positive thought. It was adopted as the Optimist International's Creed in 1922.

I had recited the creed along with my fellow Optimists for many months. One time, as I was reciting it, I thought about the way it was worded, and a light went off in my head: "Wow! We must *all* have mice in our pockets!"

It dawned on me then that the creed was written and spoken in the second person! The words "you," "yourself," or "your" are used ten times in this creed. We were all telling each other how to behave, how to think, and how to live. But we weren't programming ourselves to be optimistic!

Moreover, in that moment I realized nobody was listening! We were just speaking the words out of habit—and perhaps hoping they would stick and cause each of us to become the person those words described.

See for yourself—look at the Optimist Creed shown on the next page. You will recognize the second-person words immediately from the way it starts: "Promise Yourself." Take a moment to read each statement of the creed to see what I mean.

The Optimist Creed

Promise Yourself—

To be so strong that nothing can disturb your peace of mind.

To talk health, happiness, and prosperity to every person you meet.

To make all your friends feel that there is something in them.

To look at the sunny side of everything and make your optimism come true.

To think only of the best, to work only for the best, and to expect only the best.

To be just as enthusiastic about the success of others as you are about your own.

To forget the mistakes of the past and press on to the greater achievements of the future.

To wear a cheerful countenance at all times and give every living creature you meet a smile.

To give so much time to the improvement of yourself that you have no time to criticize others.

To be too large for worry, too noble for anger, too strong for fear, and too happy to permit the presence of trouble.

It seemed to me that if I were going to truly accept the thoughts communicated by this creed and make it a part of my life, then I had to talk to me, not to somebody else. I had to tell me how to behave, to think, and to live. It's like when I recite the Pledge of Allegiance to our flag. I, Anton Zellmann, am making the pledge to myself. I'm not telling someone else to do it.

So, I decided to edit the Optimist Creed by replacing second-person words with first-person words. I set to work replacing the word "you" with the word "I" in every sentence in the creed that contained it. Similarly, I replaced the word "your" with "my." Finally, I replaced the word "yourself" with "myself" throughout the creed.

When I sat back and read over what I had done, I experienced a very different feeling than I had when I read the original version with the second-person words. In reading the original version, I felt like an observer, like I was telling someone else what to do. But when I read my revised version, I felt like I was talking to me, and I owned what I was telling myself.

Try it for yourself and notice what you experience. The result of my editing is displayed below. Please take this moment to again read the words of each sentence of the creed in its original form (the left column) and then contrast it to the first-person form (the column on the right). As you read both versions, notice the difference in the connection you feel to the thoughts behind the words. Look at the two versions and see if the first-person version has meaning that is more personal for you, like it does for me. See if you feel more ownership over it.

The Optimist Creed

Second-Person:	First-Person:
Promise Yourself:	I Promise Myself:
To be so strong that nothing can disturb your peace of mind.	I am so strong that nothing can disturb my peace of mind.
To talk health, happiness, and prosperity to every person you meet.	To talk health, happiness, and prosperity to every person I meet.
To make all your friends feel that there is something in them.	To make all my friends feel that there is something in them.
To look at the sunny side of everything and make your optimism come true.	To look at the sunny side of everything and make my optimism come true.
To think only of the best, to work only for the best, and to expect only the best.	To think only of the best, to work only for the best, and to expect only the best.
To be just as enthusiastic about the success of others as you are about your own.	To be just as enthusiastic about the success of others as I am about my own.
To forget the mistakes of the past and press on to the greater achievements of the future.	To forget my mistakes of the past and press on to my greater achievements of the future.
To wear a cheerful countenance at all times and give every living creature you meet a smile.	To wear a cheerful countenance at all times and give every living creature I meet a smile.
To give so much time to the improvement of yourself that you have no time to criticize others.	To give so much time to the improvement of myself that I will have no time to criticize others.
To be too large for worry, too noble for anger, too strong for fear, and too happy to permit the presence of trouble.	To be too large for worry, too noble for anger, too strong for fear, and too happy to permit the presence of trouble.

I believe this comparison truly illustrates the essence of the I/You Concept. Simply put, when I talk about my feelings or actions in the second person, that is to say when I use the words "you" or "your" when it would be more appropriate to use the words "I," "me," or "my," it means I am not taking ownership of those feelings or actions. **When I talk about my feelings or actions in the first person, I am taking ownership of my feelings and my actions.**

Here's an example of the second person, describing how I felt and acted in the face of an approaching tornado: "You know—you get frightened to death, and you take cover in the first place you can find below ground."

Here's that same description in the first person: "I was frightened to death! I took cover in the first place I could find below ground!"

Notice the difference? Second-person speaking (or thinking) puts my feelings and actions "out there," away from myself, not part of me—no ownership.

When I speak (or think) in the first person, my feelings and actions are mine, part of me—I own them.

This whole notion of speaking in first person rather than second person really intrigued me. I began paying more attention to the words I was using. I noticed I was almost always speaking in second person. And so was everyone else!

Hmmm . . . What did this mean? Why did I speak and think in second person? What effect did this have on my life? How did I learn this way of speaking?

Why did I sometimes use "I" and other times "you"? Why would I sometimes be speaking in first person and then switch to second person? What benefits could I derive if I consciously replaced "you" with "I" wherever it is appropriate for me to do so?

As I thought about these questions, it occurred to me that more often than not, for whatever reason, when I spoke to people and was revealing something about myself, I inadvertently spoke mostly in second person. Moreover, I was doing this at least 90 percent of the time.

And I know as you, the reader of this book, go through this day and listen to yourself speak—and listen to other people speak—you will hear both you and others say "you" when all of you really are talking about "self."

Parental Messages

Well, why do we all do this? I believe there are several reasons.

To begin with, the parent figures in my life told me not to be egotistical: "Stop saying I did this or I did that—don't boast so much! People will think you are a braggart! People will say you are conceited! Be more humble!"

I was also taught not to be selfish. "Stop thinking so much about yourself! Everything is what *you* want! People will think you are too self-centered. It's time you started thinking about other people for a change!"

You can see the results of these "don't-use-the-words-I-or-me" messages when others around us not only do not use the first person; they don't even use the second person! They simply omit any reference to anybody! For example, I've lost count of the number of times I've heard someone say something like: "Went downtown today. Got some new shoes. Sure like the way they look!"

I was also cautioned by the parent figures in my life to not be too vulnerable. "Don't stand out in the crowd. Don't make waves. Children should be seen, not heard. Be more private.

Stop wearing your heart on your sleeve. You'll get your feelings hurt if you get too close."

These were the most insidious messages of all. They taught me if I become too intimate, someone could really hurt me. They warned me there are all kinds of people out there lurking to take advantage of me!

This "programming" of my thinking determined my scripts. I absorbed it. It is a part of who I have become and who I am. All those around me, then and now, are models for who I am. I have been and am being modeled by all of the programming passed down to me from my ancestors, by the institutions I attend, by the books I read, by movies and television programs I view, by the radio programs I hear, and even by the music to which I listen.

Protecting Myself

Of all of the various messages I was given during my programming, I believe the message about vulnerability is one of the most universal in our society, especially during our peer-pressured adolescence. Think about the forces driving this message our way. For example, I was taught to be aware of how others see me, to project an image that would make it difficult for people to think poorly of me, to sell myself. Also, I grew up in a broken home and saw divorce all around me—the message to me was, "Be careful of relationships!" And so on.

I constantly notice how much people speak in second person when they "get personal," when they are about to reveal their own thoughts, their personal perspectives on things, their personal opinions, their own perceptions of others and events, and their personal experiences.

In these many instances, I even hear people beginning their conversations with "I" statements—but then they almost instantly shift to "you" statements when their content becomes more personal, more intimate. They avoid being—or at least they don't want to be seen as—too vulnerable.

Somewhere along the way, I learned using second person words was a way for me to protect myself against my vulnerability. Second-person words distance others from me in my interactions with them. This keeps me safe from their gaining intimate knowledge about who I think I am.

I believe there is a strong element of truth about this for all of us. If I am only speaking in second person, I am camouflaging who and what I am and can be because I feel vulnerable. I am shutting out 90 percent of who I can become by simply being like everyone else.

My vulnerability could be as simple as my worrying about being seen as conceited or selfish, or as strong as seeing other people poised to hurt me because of what they know about me.

In the field of psychology today, there is a school of thought called evolutionary psychology. Proponents of this field of thought, buttressed by the recent decades of genetic research, argue many of our drives are "hard wired." One of the most important of these is our drive to protect ourselves.

As I grew up, filled with parental messages about an unsafe world and my own vulnerability living in it, I had to find ways of protecting myself. Since what I think and how those thoughts lead me to perceive my world affects what I will then feel, it's no wonder I learned to use my language as part of the protection.

Unfortunately, this self-protection habit, this lifelong programming, has terrible side effects. It sure didn't help me develop healthy relationships! I've fumbled through some pretty unhealthy associations in my life. And it sure didn't fill me with tons of self-confidence. I struggled for years to overcome feelings of being one-down from everybody else. Yeah, I was assertive, even pushy, and aggressive—but it wasn't coming from self-confidence. I was protecting myself.

It has taken me years to learn my I/You lesson, and shift my thinking and talking from second person to first person. Even today, I catch myself slipping back from time to time.

I'm finally relating to people with more comfort and confidence because I'm no longer afraid to be vulnerable. I'm finally in a wonderfully healthy relationship with my wife, Lois, because I am no longer worried about being hurt. And I've freed myself from those negative thoughts and behaviors that kept me from achieving a level of success that deep down I knew I was capable of achieving.

Thinking Outside My Small Box

So where does all of this discussion lead me? What am I advising? Am I telling people to stop using second-person references altogether?

No, it's not that simple. There are many times when it is perfectly appropriate to speak in second-person language. For example, when I ask you to do something like read the Optimist Creed or try this or that memory exercise.

When I talk about the I/You Concept, I am referring only to those moments when I am speaking about myself. When I am revealing who I am, what I am, what I think, what I believe, how I live, how I behave.

It is that part of living that I encourage others to notice and change. It has worked and is working for me, and I know it will work for you.

This means doing something I will talk about in several places in this book—it means, "thinking outside my box."

The habits I developed over the years, the scripts I learned and adapted as my own, were always comfortable to me, even when they didn't work for me. When I work at changing them and try some new behaviors, I experience discomfort. Fortunately, that discomfort lasts only a little while. Over time, the new behaviors gradually replace the old habits, and I have a new sense of comfort.

Thus, when it comes to the I/You Concept, my advice to myself and to you is for each of us to make a conscious decision to take charge of our behavior by shifting our language from second to first person when talking about our personal selves. This will help us begin to own what we think, what we say, and what we do.

Once I made that commitment to myself, I began training myself to be constantly aware of when I use the second person as I talk about myself. To this day, every time I notice it happen, I pause and examine my feelings at that moment. It's amazing how many times I find vulnerability involved.

The miraculous part of it is I begin to hear (please allow me for effect to use a bit of street language here) the B.S. that comes out of me. I hear the statements I make that I no longer accept. I hear statements I make that even when I was a child, if I had thought about it, I would not have accepted.

And it's important for me to note that I do not use these instances as opportunities to punish myself. It would be so easy to think something like: "There I go again! How stupid!" But it would be very self-defeating.

In chapter 6, I will relay information about the "self-fulfilling prophecy," which essentially means, "As I think, so shall I become." Negative self-messages really hurt me in the long run.

So, instead of punishing myself, I objectively study myself at those moments when I observe myself using second instead of first-person language. I examine my feelings and challenge the premises on which they are based. I am not going to be hurt. They are not going to see me as dumb, stupid, conceited, selfish, etc. Better yet, even if they do, it does not matter, because I know I am not any of those things.

I then repeat the second-person statement with a first-person statement. And I tell myself now I truly own it!

The more I open myself up in this way, the more confident and relaxed I become. And the more open and comfortable others become with me.

It's All about Change!

Changing my thinking and speaking from second to first-person language meant I had to challenge my earlier notions about change. I discovered I had been viewing change as a threat. Every time a change came about I felt threatened.

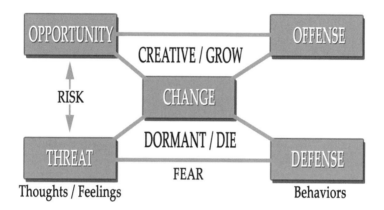

But I then learned threat is really just a feeling, a feeling that probably started early in my life. I remember many instances early in my life when change was threatening to me.

I remember what now seems like a very simple little instance when I was a kid, about five years old. My first stepfather (I had four) was experiencing some heart problems. My mom couldn't handle all the pressure on her so she placed my brother Richard and me in a foster home. I remember being taught some of my "early programming" in that home.

I felt abandoned when on visiting day my mom didn't come to see me. I can recall feeling very lonely when other kids got mail from home and I didn't. I can vividly recall being taught how to tie my shoes. Picture what I am about to describe. It really happened. The lady of the house said to me, "OK, little Joey, it's time you learned to tie your own shoes. And when you learn how to tie your shoes, you can put both hands in that bowl of candy and have all you can hold on to!"

I recall it was a bowl of M&Ms, and I sure wanted some!

So I learned to tie my shoes. Looking back, I'm not sure if it took me a day or a month or a couple of hours. But, however long it took me to learn, I did learn to tie my shoes. This was a big deal for me as a little kid. And at first it was very difficult to accomplish.

But accomplish it I did. I ran over to the bowl of M&Ms. The lady stopped me in my tracks and said, "Not yet. I will let you have some after you show my husband how you can tie your shoes."

Well, when he got there, I think it was probably the first time I was in show business. Honest to goodness, this is what happened. She said to her husband: "Look at little Joey tie his shoes. Come on, Joey, show us how you can do it!"

I got down on one of my little knees, and I tied one shoe and then the other. I did the best I could do. It might not have been perfect, but I tied my shoes.

To my surprise, the guy just looked at me and didn't say anything. He simply left the room. After a few moments, he returned and said, "Let me show you a different way to do that."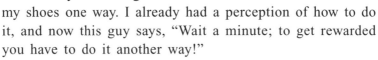

Ooh! Change! I reacted to it! I had already been taught how to tie my shoes one way. I already had a perception of how to do it, and now this guy says, "Wait a minute; to get rewarded you have to do it another way!"

And so I behaved defensively. Because that's what I do—as I think most human beings do—when I feel threatened. And do you know what my defensive behavior was? I cried. I cried long, and I cried loud. He didn't want to put up with it. So, he did what a lot of parents might do today. He left the room.

I then made a beeline for the candy. I got what I wanted. And unconsciously, I reinforced a habit I had probably begun learning in my crib—and some would say even in my mother's womb. I learned the habit of responding defensively.

Consequently, every time I wanted to get my way, I cried. I cried whenever I got angry. I did this well into my thirties. I unconsciously thought crying would help me get what I wanted. I cried so much along the way one of my stepfathers called me Bubbles. And of course that didn't go down so well. It wasn't until years later I understood defensive behavior may get me what I want at the moment, but it rarely works in the long run.

Again, it's all about change. And change can be very risky. Why? It comes back to making myself vulnerable.

Once I trained myself to open up and realized it was perfectly OK for me to be vulnerable, that people were not out to take advantage of me, that I could defend myself in other ways besides crying or showing anger, I then began to bring to me all kinds of exciting and rewarding experiences.

I developed a keener awareness of things happening to me and to others around me.

I became more sensitive, more tuned into my own feelings and the feelings of others.

I became more open to experimentation, to new experiences, to creativity, and yes, even to change.

I also became more accepting of my intuition as a bona fide sense.

In the following chapters, I plan to share information and exercises designed to help you to experience the same wonderful changes I have experienced and am still experiencing.

Reading and Thinking in the First Person

I'm going to reinforce the I/You Concept and your staying in the first person as much as I can throughout this book in order to encourage you to take ownership of what you read. I

THE I/YOU CONCEPT: BEYOND MY SELF-TALK

will do this by using as much "first-person language" throughout as I can.

Recall my earlier example of second-person speaking, using a description of how I felt and acted in the face of an approaching tornado: "You know—you get frightened to death, and you take cover in the first place you can find below ground."

Remember that same description in the first person: "I was frightened to death! I took cover in the first place I could find below ground!"

Notice how the second-person language depersonalizes what I said. More importantly, it denies my ownership of my feelings.

In contrast, the first-person statement is very personal, conveying a clear, strong sense of self. It clearly shows how much I own my own feelings!

Now read both statements aloud. Notice the difference in what you feel as you read them. I feel a little like a professor teaching his class when I read the first statement but strong and self-confident when I read the second statement.

I want to be absolutely certain I do not create any confusion about the purpose for my writing and requesting that you read this book in first person.

Naturally, there are times when it is perfectly appropriate for me to speak in second-person language. For example, when, in the following chapters I ask you, the reader of this book, to think about something, to attempt a memory technique, or to practice doing some other mental exercise, then I will phrase my statement or make my request using second person *you* instead of first person *I*.

So for clarity sake, I want you to once again note, there will be many places on the following pages where I am

41

specifically speaking about Anton's ideas, Anton's experiences, Anton's thoughts, and Anton's beliefs. And then there will be times when I am writing in the first person *I* because I am asking you to read every *I, me,* and *my* statement as if they belonged to you so *you* will be more likely to receive the impact of a particular concept or statement.

Of course there will be times when you will read an *I* statement that obviously refers not only to you but also to me and to everyone else as well. For example, in the next chapter I will be talking about the human brain and although many points I make are true for everyone, I will express them as first person *I* statements. My purpose will be to help to continue training you to read in first person for all of the reasons I previously described.

I believe when you read all of the first-person statements written on these pages to yourself, you will more firmly own what you learn. In fact, I strongly suggest you read all books from which you choose to learn in first person. It's amazing how easy it is to do and how much benefit can be derived!

Now it's time to share with you a variety of tools I know will help you better understand and hone your mental skills. These tools have worked for me and I believe they will work for you as well.

CHAPTER FOUR

My Brain: The Nuts and Bolts of My Memory

> Music is the effort we make to explain to ourselves how our brains work. We listen to Bach transfixed because this is listening to a human mind.
> —*Lewis Thomas (1913-1993)*
> *U.S. physician, educator*

It all starts with my brain. Without my brain there would be no feeling, no thinking, no seeing, no creating, no memory. Clearly, a little knowledge of the workings of my brain is a helpful place to begin a journey to improve memory.

My brain is made up of a very large number of interconnected nerve cells called neurons. I had one hundred billion of them at birth! And, barring any unfortunate accidents along the way, I will still have about ninety-five billion of them when I grow old and die. Many years ago, I was told that to do what my brain does would take a computer the size of the Empire State Building, and all of the water flowing over Niagara Falls to cool it off. Even today, with the miniaturization of the computer chip, this statement still holds true.

This immense tangle of brain cells gives me a tremendous learning and memory capacity. In fact, the amount of information I am capable of storing in my brain would fill ten million one-thousand-page books. Wow! Even the brightest, most educated, most informed people in the world today have barely tapped their potential. Einstein was said to have used less than 10 percent of his brainpower. The rest of us use somewhere between 3 and 7 percent. Just think, this means we have at least 93 percent more brainpower into which we can tap.

How My Brain Is Wired

Let's take a closer look at the basic unit of the brain—the neuron—to see how learning takes place. Note: remembering something is a form of learning.

To begin with, neurons are composed of three parts: the cell nucleus (the center of the nerve cell), the "sending" end of the neuron known as the axon, and the "receiving" end of the neuron called the dendrite. Each end is composed of many "connectors," like branches on a tree.

The drawing below is a sketch of a neuron. Looking from left to right you see the dendrite, the cell nucleus, and the axon.

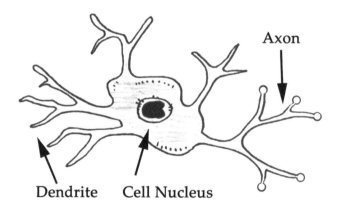

Both the dendrite and the axon of a neuron are composed of many "connectors." This means a neuron can send and receive many messages at the same time.

Now, here's where it gets interesting. When thinking takes place, a kind of electrical impulse jumps across a small gap between the two neurons from the axon of one, to the dendrite of the other:

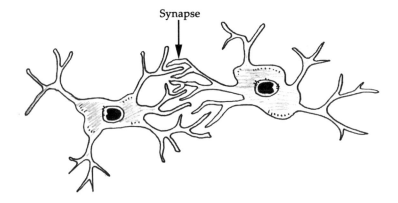

Synapse

This small gap is very important to my understanding of the nuts and bolts of memory. It is known as the synapse. Doctor Pierce J. Howard, in his fascinating book, *Owner's Manual of the Brain*, notes neurons are connected to other neurons by as many as one to ten thousand synapses. In fact, given the millions of neurons in my brain, each with thousands of synapses, it would take tens of millions of years just to count the number of synapses!

New synapses are formed, and the connectivity among neurons becomes more complex when learning takes place. The more knowledge I acquire, the greater the number of synapses and patterns of connectivity—the greater is the density of my brain.

Very important to memory is the condition of these synapses. Chemicals, known as neurotransmitters, which are secreted at the synapse, affect the activity of neurons. Drinking milk, for example, causes sleepiness because the calcium in milk triggers the secretion of a chemical called "melatonin" which activates sleep. Coffee, on the other hand, is stimulating because it blocks the relaxing effects of a neurotransmitter known as adenosine.

My psychological state, my physical condition, and my environment also affect the communication among my neurons. How stressed do I feel? How tired am I? Am I in a noisy place?

Am I depressed? Am I in physical pain? Am I in a very warm place? Am I in a brightly lit place?

In other words, many things affect the functioning of my brain and, in turn, my ability to remember. What I eat. What I feel. What I do. Where I am. I will be touching on all of these as factors influencing my memory as I move through the pages of this book.

For now, I want to take a few moments and see where memory is located in the brain and what happens when I remember something.

Memory and My Brain

I begin by looking at some important parts of the brain associated with memory. The drawing below is a rough sketch of my brain. My brain sits on top of my spinal cord. My brain stem is a collection of brain structures that connect the rest of my brain to my spinal cord. It is a kind of relay center for incoming neural messages from other parts of my body. Activities that take place in this structure have to do with the regulation of my bodily functions such as hunger, thirst, body temperature, emotions, and blood pressure. In other words, the structures making up my brain stem react to changes in both my internal and external environments, and exchanges between the two.

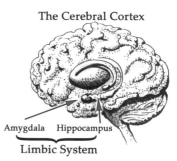

The border around the upper end of my brain stem is the limbic system. Two important parts of the limbic system for memory are the amygdala and the hippocampus. The amygdala regulates our emotions. Events associated with high emotions are important enough to become memories. The hippocampus is associated with short-term memory. People with damage in this area find it very difficult to remember recent events.

The biggest part of my brain—people years ago used to think it was the brain—is my cerebral cortex. This is the highly developed thinking part of my brain that distinguishes me from other animals. It is important for long-term memory.

A popular approach to describing memory formation is to think about pieces of memory as "chunks." When I turn my attention to something, I "capture" a memory chunk. This is referred to as immediate memory. It is very temporary—my brain is processing thousands of pieces of data in just a few seconds. When I am looking for a street as I drive, for example, I will see one street name after the other. I typically will remember each for just a second or two as I drive to the next.

When I focus my attention on something for a few seconds—one expert says eight seconds is the minimum—the immediate memory chunk is added to my short-term memory. This takes place in the hippocampus, which is my brain's mechanism for selecting chunks to remember.

Long-term memory is located in my cerebral cortex. When I think more about a short-term memory chunk and tie it to other memory chunks (as I will do with some exercises in this book), the hippocampus communicates with the cerebral cortex and establishes long-term memory. I find it fascinating that the long-term memory chunk is not just stored in one location in my brain. In fact, it is stored throughout my brain. The reason is that each memory chunk is connected to other, similar memory chunks in my brain. All of these related chunks are loosely tied together into a network of memory chunks. It's almost like my brain makes "backups" of my memory.

Four events can occur to diminish my long-term memory. First, my synapses can become "clogged," much like the way spark plugs in my car become clogged. This occurs when proteins build up on each side of the synaptic gap. Such clogging is cleaned up by a neurotransmitter named calpain, which is found in calcium.

Second, the neural pathways involved in a particular memory chunk may deteriorate. This happens when my brain fails to produce enough of the neurotransmitter, acetylcholine, which keeps the membranes of the neurons fresh and nonbrittle. My intake of fat is one of the things that will affect the production of acetylcholine in my brain—if my daily diet consistently includes less than the recommended daily allowance, the amount of acetylcholine produced will drop.

The third factor influencing my long-term memory is stress. When I am stressed, the limbic system at the top of my brain stem (short-term memory) becomes more active and my cerebral cortex (long term) less active. Thus, when I am stressed, I will find it harder to recall memories.

The fourth circumstance diminishing my long-term memory is a lower level of the neurotransmitters epinephrine and norepinephrine. Research shows lower levels of these neurotransmitters are associated with poorer recall.

Protecting My Memory with a Healthy Brain

By now you may be wondering why I'm spending all of this time talking about my brain. What does this discussion have to do with techniques for improving memory?

Well, I can come up with all kinds of mnemonic exercises for memory improvement recall, but if I don't follow some basic guidelines for keeping my brain healthy, those techniques won't do me much good.

"So," you might say, "what can I do to keep my brain healthy and insure my chances of improving my memory?"

The answer to that question lies with the neurotransmitters in my brain. Anything that influences the levels of those neurotransmitters will affect the functioning of my brain. Such influences fall into four categories: nutrition, exercise, emotional state, and stimulation.

Nutrition

The obvious place for me to start is with what and how I eat and drink. The substances I ingest provide my body with nutrients, all of which affect my health in general (which affects the functioning of my brain), and some of which directly affect neurotransmitters.

Four food groups particularly influence the way my brain functions: protein, complex carbohydrates, simple carbohydrates, and fats.

Proteins come from both animal and plant sources. Protein contains an amino acid called L-tyrosine. When I ingest protein, the L-tyrosine produces the neurotransmitters norepinephrine and dopamine. The effect is I feel more alert and analytical. So when I'm about to engage in an activity that requires me to be alert and analytical, I eat some protein.

According to some experts, the recommended daily intake is about eight grams per kilogram of your body weight. That would be about a 1.7-ounce hamburger patty for a 180-pound person.

Complex carbohydrates are found in a variety of fruit, vegetables, and grains. If I'm feeling anxious or tense, I eat such foods—they contain an amino acid known as L-tryptophan. L-tryptophan produces serotonin, which gives me a sense of relaxation. Nutritionists recommend carbohydrates make up about 55 percent of a person's daily calorie intake.

Simple carbohydrates are found in sugars. Like complex carbohydrates, they produce alertness—they act as an energy booster, producing glucose. However, ingesting simple carbohydrates alone does not have as lasting an effect as ingesting complex carbohydrates—after the burst of energy, I am likely to feel very sluggish.

Incidentally, research has shown that the order of protein and carbohydrate intake is important. The French who have their salads after the main course may have it right. If I want to be more alert after eating, I should eat my protein first in order to get the L-tyrosine into my brain first, which perks me up. Then, I eat my carbohydrates. This will give me an energy release without sleepiness or letdown.

Fats are found in dairy, meat, and various oils. Recall that every time I remember something, I am building up the synaptic networks in my brain. Fats are especially important to this process because they stimulate the production of acetylcholine, which strengthens neural membranes.

In addition to these food groups, vitamins B and C are important to brain function. In particular, B6 will heighten my brainpower. This vitamin is found in a variety of meats, including pork, liver, and chicken, and in whole wheat bread, cereals, and nuts. Vitamin C enhances my brain's use of proteins to help me develop that synaptic network that makes up my memory.

Aerobic Exercise

The importance of aerobic exercise to the functioning of my brain cannot be overestimated. Any exercise stimulates my nervous system, especially aerobic exercise. Aerobic exercise increases the growth of axons, which, after all, are critical to the communication between neurons in my brain.

Aerobic exercise stimulates the release of the neurotransmitters called endorphins. These neurotransmitters create more alertness in the cortex of my brain. Aerobic exercise also leads to a greater abundance of neurotriphins, which help my neurons to grow. Finally, as a result of aerobic exercise, more capillaries form around my neurons. This facilitates more blood, and thus more oxygen reaching my brain.

What all of this means for memory is that aerobic exercise will improve the quality of my mental functioning, as well as the amount and speed of my recall.

Test this out. Try some of the memory exercises presented later in this book before engaging in a session of aerobic exercise and then try some after the session. Most likely there will be a difference in memory effectiveness.

By the way, when I'm talking about aerobic exercise, I'm talking about a nonstop physical activity that keeps my heart pumping higher for at least fifteen to twenty minutes.

Caution: If you have not been regularly exercising, check with your doctor before you begin exerting yourself. And don't plunge yourself into it too fast, too hard, or too soon! Phase yourself into it and gradually build up your pace and time.

Emotional State

Happier, more optimistic people usually have less trouble staying alert. Depressed or pessimistic people are more lethargic. My mood will definitely affect my alertness. At the same time, my level of alertness (recall our discussion of nutrition) will affect my mood.

People who are depressed for long periods of time will be less successful at remembering. Depression is associated with low energy and tension. I can counteract depression in two ways: the right balance of foods, particularly protein and carbohydrates, and aerobic exercise. For all of the reasons mentioned on previous pages, these will stimulate more alertness and energy. (I'm not referring here to deep, clinical depression. That might call for more extensive medical and therapeutic measures.)

Research also has shown laughter leads to more alertness. Continued laughter, the deeper the better, increases respiration (much like aerobic exercise), which leads to an increase of endorphins and thus more cortical alertness. (Incidentally, a nice side effect of laughter is an increase in the number of my immune cells.) That's why I make laughter a particularly important part of my day!

My most debilitating emotional state is when I am feeling stressed. Stress leads to a redistribution of my blood away from my brain to my heart and other muscles. This is because my body automatically prepares itself for attack. This leads to a drop in the production of new neurons—after all, my body is busy elsewhere. I will certainly have more difficulty trying to remember things when I am stressed.

There are many things I can do to overcome stress. Basic relaxation, such as sitting quietly and breathing steadily and easily, naps, meditation, and all-out sleep will help reduce stress. Once again, aerobic exercise is effective in reducing stress. Laughter reduces stress. Psychotherapy, in which I learn to reframe the way I look at the world, helps me reduce long-term stress.

Stimulation

Finally, I come to "stimulating my brain." At the risk of sounding trite or corny, let me say—and I can't shout this loud enough—*use it or lose it!* The more I use my brain, the more alert I am and the better my chances at improving my memory.

Years ago, when scientists looked at research data, they concluded mental alertness decreases with age. But current researchers are finding one particular variable was not taken into account: how much a person used his or her brain.

Using my brain in learning, reading, thinking, creating, and such is exercising my brain. As physical exercise builds up my muscles, mental exercise increases the number of synapses and neural networks in my brain. In fact, when comparing the brain scans of older people who were socially and mentally active to  other older people who were not very active, researchers found the brains of the first group were denser with synaptic connections. One might even say their brains were actually growing—as compared to the second group.

In a Harvard medical school study, researchers found a group of physicians over age sixty-five who measured high on cognitive skills were still actively working as compared to a group of physicians with the lowest scores who were not working.

There is no question about it: When considering my memory ability, *I must use it or lose it!* I provide several exercises in the next two chapters designed to help to "use it."

CHAPTER FIVE

NLP: A Window to My Thinking

If everybody is thinking alike, then somebody isn't thinking.
—*George S. Patton Jr. (1885-1945)*
General, United States Army

Getting to know about my brain was only a first step for me. It was even more helpful to learn how my brain, my internal world, is connected to my outside world. Although I had not consciously planned it, once again the right information came along at just the right time.

In 1976 I signed up for a training that introduced me to some helpful techniques in the field of Neuro-Linguistic Programming, known as NLP, to help me do this. These techniques took me to the next level of memory improvement. More than that, these are techniques that helped me sharpen my mental abilities in general. They opened the door to greater self-discovery, improved communication, and enriched relationships. But hold on a minute. I'm getting ahead of myself.

First developed by Richard Bandler and John Grinder, NLP is the study of the associations between thinking, language, and behavior. Bandler was a mathematician working in the field of information science—a computer programmer. Grinder was a linguist. Together, they were interested in studying people who were excellent communicators and people who easily and successfully adapted to change. Among the successful people they studied were well-known therapists, linguists, anthropologists, and psychoanalysts. The results of their efforts led them to construct a model of the way the mind works. They called their model NLP. This model is based on the realization that I create much of my experience by the specific ways I see, hear, and feel things in my mind/body—what is usually lumped together and called "thinking." Using NLP techniques helps me to sharpen my thinking. Bandler says most people are prisoners of their own brains. It would be like being chained to the last seat of a bus I'm not driving. If I want to learn how to drive my own bus, I need to give my brain direction. I need to sharpen and shape my own thinking.

For example, I always thought having a "photographic memory" was an inborn talent. I wished I had one. The fact is, I do have a photographic memory and didn't even know it. To demonstrate, suppose I've just gone to a great movie. I am now home. I'm sitting in my chair and describing this great movie to someone else. As I describe a scene, I can see it in my "mind's eye." I bet everyone has had that sort of experience at one time or another!

See? I do have a photographic memory, and so do you! It seems that most people just haven't trained themselves to use it in a focused way. They just haven't learned how to give their brains the appropriate direction. Most people spend more time learning how to use gadgets like a VCR, a camera, or a computer than they do learning how to use their brains more effectively. NLP helps me learn how to use my brain in ways that are more functional.

The "Neuro" in Neuro-Linguistic Programming refers to my neurological system. In particular, it refers to the connections in my brain between my senses—seeing, hearing, touching, tasting, and smelling—and the way I think and experience the world around me.

The "Linguistic" in Neuro-Linguistic Programming refers to my language patterns—both the way I think and how I use those thoughts to communicate to others and to shape my experiences.

The "Programming" in Neuro-Linguistic Programming refers to how I "code" my experiences. The concept comes from computer programming. A computer program consists of many lines of "code" designed to accomplish a task. Without realizing it, I grew into adulthood developing many "programs"—thinking "blueprints"—I use to both interpret and describe my experience, to myself and to others.

The more I am aware of my neurological processes—the connections between my senses and the way I think—the more I will become aware of how I think. And the more I become aware of how I think, the more I will become aware of the kinds of programming I developed over the years—programming that determines my choices and experiences in life to this very day.

Three Kinds of Thinking Processes

Consider that my senses of sight, hearing, touch, taste, and smell are the means—the pathways—for me to get information into my brain. My preference for one or a combination of these pathways is reflected in the way I think.

This results in three major kinds of thinking: visual, auditory, and kinesthetic.

I am visually thinking when I think in terms of pictures. For example, when someone asks me about the house I used to live in, I tap my memory of that house in terms of a picture. I see the house in my mind, the brick siding, the green front door, the bushes, and colorful flowers in front of the living room window. I see the walk winding its way up to my front door.

I am engaged in auditory thinking when I think in terms of sounds. For example, if I am asked about my trip to the Indianapolis 500, the first thing that comes to my mind is the loud, roaring sound of race cars, the screeching of tires, and the discordant sound of vehicles crashing into each other and into the walls along the side of the speedway.

I am engaged in kinesthetic thinking when I think in terms of my feelings or physical sensations such as touch, taste, and smell. For example, if I am asked about a new restaurant I recently experienced, I can smell the wonderful odors wafting out from the kitchen, taste the delicious food I had, and recall the comfortable sensation of the padded chairs and the total feeling of enjoyment I experienced.

Each of us has a preference for one or a combination of these thinking processes. Learning about those preferences, both our own preferences and those of others, will help us in many areas of our lives—areas such as improving our memory, our communication skills, our relationships, and our personal and professional success. And yes, even to read the minds of others.

A good personal example of how this knowledge can help relationships is when I first met my wife, Lois. I was feeling very unloved and very insecure, having just come out of a devastating breakup of my first marriage. I was desperate to hear from Lois (or anyone for that matter) that she loved me. Of course, she constantly demonstrated her love to me. But she had never said it to me. Then one day, she left a message on my answering machine and finished it with those tender, magical words, "I love you." It gave me so much joy to hear those words because—as I now know—my primary modality is auditory, and to get the message, I need to hear the words. So, perhaps childishly, I copied the recording onto a small tape recorder and listened to it every time I needed to hear it (about ten times a day).

We talked and laughed about that incident over the years. It wasn't until recently we came to understand that Lois doesn't need to hear "I love you" because her primary modality is kinesthetic—it's demonstrated by my actions. She feels it. She doesn't have to hear it. But, being auditory, I need to hear it as often as possible. So today, aware of our differences, we know how to "feed" each other's modality. I consciously demonstrate my love with my actions, and she speaks those precious words to me often.

Learning My Own Preferred Thinking Processes

It all starts with my learning about my own preferred thinking process. To help me do this, I devised a five-item test.

I will present five numbered statements, each followed by three possible reactions to the statement. For each statement, circle the one letter in the left column that best fits your strongest reaction to the statement.

The statements (shown in shadowed boxes) with several possible reactions are presented below and on the next page:

1.	Think about the last time you had dinner with friends at a good restaurant...
A	I immediately have a vivid mental picture of myself having dinner with my friends—their faces, the table setting, the dishware, and the bottle of wine.
B	I immediately hear the signs of people talking around me, of silverware tinkling on plates, and of quiet music playing.
C	I immediately remember the smells of food in the restaurant and the taste of my own meal and drink.
2.	Think about yourself standing in front of a pump at a gas station...
A	A picture comes to my mind of the gas pump with its window and hose and the other pumps around it.
B	I hear the sound of the gasoline rushing into the tank of my car and the sounds of other cars coming and going from the gas station.
C	I smell gasoline and feel my hand on the pump as I fill the gas tank in my car.
3.	Think about yourself at a checkout stand in a grocery store...
A	I easily see the checkout counter, the clerk behind it, my groceries on the conveyor belt, and the people around me in the store.
B	I immediately hear the sounds of my groceries being placed in bags, the sound of the cash register as the clerk totals my purchase, and the sounds of other people talking at their registers.
C	I can easily feel myself lifting cans and other items from my grocery cart and putting them on the counter and then pushing the empty cart forward as I prepare to pay for my groceries.

4.	Think about yourself coming out of a meeting with a group of people…
A	I can easily recall what each person was wearing—the colors and patterns of their clothes, what their ties looked like, and so forth.
B	I can easily recall who said what and what was said—I can easily replay in my head the conversations that took place.
C	I can easily recall such sensations as the feel of my body settled in the chair on which I was sitting and the feel of the pencil in my hand as I took notes.
5.	Think about yourself driving through a fast-food take-out place like McDonald's…
A	I immediately see myself driving into the driveway, seeing cars ahead of me in line, and looking at the posted menu, etc.
B	I easily hear the sound of my car, the sound of the window going down, the voice of someone asking me for my order, and the sound of my voice as I place my order.
C	I easily feel my hands on the steering wheel as I come to the pick-up window, and I smell the strong odors of hamburgers and french fries.

Now count the number of *A*s, *B*s, and *C*s you circled. Which letter did you circle most?

If you circled mostly *A*s, your most preferred thinking process is probably visual.

If you circled mostly *B*s, your most preferred thinking process is probably auditory.

If you circled mostly *C*s, your most preferred thinking process is probably kinesthetic.

If you circled a mixture of letters, you may have a combination of preferred thinking processes.

Don't be surprised if your preferred thinking process is visual. Research has shown more than half of us prefer the visual thinking process.

Learning the Preferred Thinking Processes of Others

I can also learn about the preferred thinking patterns of others. NLP experts have discovered I can do this by watching a person's eye movements. Different eye movements are associated with different mental processes—different ways of thinking. I can even learn a person's preferred pattern by asking questions that include specific words like: look, feel, or sound.

The main mental processes linked to eye movements are known as:

Looking to My Left	Looking to My Right
Visual Constructed	Visual Remembered
Auditory Constructed	Auditory Remembered
Kinesthetic (Feelings)	Kinesthetic (Self-Talk)

Keep in mind I am observing a person's eyes from *my point of view*, not theirs. So when I say the person is looking to my right, he or she is actually looking to their left.

*For clarity, I will be speaking here of the eye movements as I look out through **my eyes**.* Noticing the other person's eye movements gives me clues as to how he or she is thinking.

For example, when I notice people looking **up** to my **left** (their right), they are probably imagining things they've never seen before or picturing things they've seen in a different way. This is called visual constructed. Here are some things you might say that would elicit a visual-constructed process. "Think what a bright pink Cadillac would look like." "Imagine how you look if you were two feet taller and sixty pounds heavier." "Picture yourself flying like Superman above the Washington Monument."

If I see someone looking **sideways** to my **left** (their right), they are probably imagining sounds they've never heard before or hearing familiar sounds in a different way than they usually hear them. This is called auditory constructed. Here are some questions that may stimulate this auditory-constructed process. "If you and a friend were singing happy birthday together, what would it sound like?" "What would you hear if you were at the bottom of the ocean in a submarine?"

When I see a person looking **down** and to my **left** (their right), chances are they are feeling emotions, or they are experiencing the sensations of muscle movements as they would in some kind of actual physical movement. This mental process is called kinesthetic. The following questions would stimulate this kinesthetic mental process. "What does it feel like to be very angry?" "What does it feel like to jump across a puddle of water?" "What does it feel like to sit in a bathtub filled with warm water?"

When I notice people looking **up** to my **right** (their left), I know they are probably searching their minds for visual information that is stored away. This is called visual remembered. It means they are searching their memories for things they've seen before in the same way they were seen before. They are visually remembering.

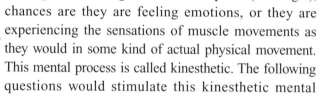

Here are some questions that may elicit this kind of mental processing. "Think about your first car—what color was it?" "Think about having dinner last night. What color were the dishes on the table? Describe what the main course looked like."

When I am looking at people while they are searching for sounds they have heard in the past, I see them looking **sideways** to my **right** (their left). This is called auditory remembered. The following questions may elicit this kind of mental processing. "What does rain sound like?" "What does a foghorn sound like?" "What does heavy rain sound like?" "What does the 'Star-Spangled Banner' sound like?"

When I am watching a person and he is looking **down** to my **right** (his left), he is probably talking to himself in his mind. This mental process is called self-talk. Here are some examples of statements that would elicit this kind of processing. "Say something to yourself you often say to yourself." "Think about yourself delivering Lincoln's Gettysburg Address." "Recall a nursery rhyme you used to recite when you were a child."

Eye-Accessing Cues

All six of these eye movements are clues about what the other person is thinking. Because they give me access to the other person's thoughts, I refer to them as "eye-accessing cues."

The table below is a summary of how eye-accessing cues—eye movements—are connected to the preferred thinking patterns of an individual as I look at that person through my eyes.

Eye Accessing Cue	Eye Movement	Eye Accessing Cue	Eye Movement
Visual Constructed *Imagining Sights*	Up to My Left	Visual Remembered *Recalling Sights*	Up to My Right
Auditory Constructed *Imagining Sounds*	Sideways to My Left	Auditory Remembered *Recalling Sounds*	Sideways to My Right
Kinesthetic *Feeling Emotions*	Down to My Left	Kinesthetic *Engaging in Self-talk*	Down to My Right

This knowledge is also very useful in everyday situations with people. Making use of it helps me listen to and communicate with others more effectively. It will also help me more accurately store and recall conversations and interactions. For example, suppose I am a doctor who is interviewing a patient.

Let's say I am primarily an auditory thinker, and my patient is a visual thinker. I conduct my interview, I make my observations, and I conclude a particular regimen will be of benefit to my patient's health.

I explain to the patient what I want him or her to do and for how long. I might even be heard to conclude my visit with the words, "Now don't forget to take your medicine three times a day, every day with your meals—understand?"

"Sure I will," says the patient, who most likely is already in a dither over her condition and anxious about having to remember to take her medicine.

Well, I can tell you if, as I described, she is visual and I am auditory, there is a good chance she may not have gotten the message at all, or at least will be more likely to forget it before she gets out the door.

On the other hand, what if I understood my patient was visual and I was auditory? Then I would know it was important to show her something visual that could best convey my communication. I might use a visual aid or my script pad, or the face of a clock—anything that provides some visual support. I could also ask her at what time during the day she might take the pills to give her an opportunity to "see herself" taking the pills.

Suppose the patient returns to my office, and I see she hasn't done as well as I thought she should have. I suspect the next thing I might do is to interview her to learn what's going on. "Mrs. Brown, did you take your medication three times a day with your meals as I prescribed?"

Now I can watch her eyes, which will give me a good clue as to whether or not she did as I asked. For instance, if she immediately looks up and sideways to my right, there's a good chance she did what I told her. Why? Because looking right means she is remembering stored sights and sounds.

On the other hand, if she looks up or sideways to my left, she probably is a bit confused about her answer. Why? Because looking up or sideways to the left means she is trying to imagine sights or sounds. This might give me cause to want to continue the interview to determine if she did as I asked.

Like most techniques, there is no guarantee this application of NLP will absolutely work 100 percent of the time. But I have found it to be a very helpful technique. I hope you will try it. Please e-mail me at anton@zellmannpublishing.com and tell me about your experiences. Every time I hear from someone, I learn a little more. It then gives me new opportunities to share what I have learned with others.

My Memory

Given, as NLP experts tell us, that I connect my visual, auditory, and kinesthetic sensory experiences to my thinking, it's an easy step to the notion these thinking modalities have something to do with my memory. It turns out there are three principal kinds of memory: visual, verbal (auditory), and kinesthetic.

Consider *verbal memory*. When I say a word or hear someone speak a word that signifies an object, and it brings up the sound of that object, I probably have a good verbal memory. My guess would be I would have no difficulty imagining the scenes described in stories I hear and read.

Then there is *visual memory*. When I recall my experience as a child in elementary school, do I quickly see images of my classroom and the school and other students? If I easily do so, I probably have good visual memory.

Finally, there is kinesthetic memory. Here, I am talking about my senses and my emotions.

My senses are strongly linked to my memory. For instance, the scent of cotton candy takes me right back to Coney Island and being eight years old. It causes me to think of corn on the cob dripping with melted butter, the Steeple Chase rides, and putting coins in the machines in the penny arcade.

My emotions are also linked to my memory—almost any emotion from joy to sadness can evoke a childhood memory. When I think about being afraid or angry or sad, experiences of being angry or sad from my past pop into my mind. I bet that happens to you too!

For example, I heard a piece of music during a very trying period when I was young that for years afterward evoked feelings of melancholy. Of course, at the time I first heard the music, I didn't know about NLP. But over the years, when I felt downhearted hearing the music, I began to realize the connection.

The music was Eddie Calvert playing "Cherry Pink & Apple Blossom White." I was about nine or ten years old when I first heard it at a friend's house. He had his radio on while we were playing a game. I enjoyed it and just couldn't get it out of my thinking.

Meanwhile, my mother and my second stepfather, with whom I was living in Brooklyn, battled all the time. They just couldn't get along. One night, they had a huge fight, physically harmful to both of them. I was lying in bed, trying not to hear them. I recall thinking I would never get married (fortunately the vow didn't last), and I decided I had to do something to stop them from hurting each other.

While all of this was happening, I was listening to music on my radio to try and drown out the battle. Yes, you guessed it. "Cherry Pink & Apple Blossom White" was playing. I tried to get them to stop fighting, but they wouldn't. So, I ran out of the house to a police station down the block to get help. It was a sad time. It was sad to have to listen to two adults constantly fighting and hurting one another. It was sad to have to call a policeman into my private home to see how my folks behaved.

Years later, when I began learning about NLP material and realized how auditory I am, I finally understood the connection between the music and my history. Everything going on at that horrible moment in my life—my anguish, my embarrassment, my helplessness—was connected and anchored to that Eddie Calvert piece of music. It's no wonder I would feel sad when hearing it.

However, the more I have come to understand these kinds of memory connections, the more I have come to realize I do not have to feel sad when I hear that music. The connection represents history. That was then, and this is now. I can now listen to that song and do not have to feel bad. I am in control of me. The more I realize the influence of such early memory connections, the more I gain control over my own life, the more empowered I become.

In our everyday living, when we remember past experiences, most of us probably favor one of these three principal kinds of memory: verbal, visual, or kinesthetic.

NLP: A Window to My Thinking

For example, suppose I decide to paint my kitchen. I write down a list of the various supplies and tools I need to pick up from the hardware store. As I am driving to the store, do I repeat the list of items in my mind? That's verbal memory. Or do I more easily see the objects I want to buy? That's visual memory. Or do the smell of paint and the sensation of my slapping paint on the wall come to my mind as I think about the things I want to buy? That's kinesthetic memory.

Although you probably already have a good idea of your preferred memory strategy from the self-test you took a few pages back, I would like to offer another brief quiz to help you further identify it. For each statement in the table below, close your eyes for a few seconds and try to experience what the statement describes. Then, in the column to the right of the statement, rate how hard it was for you to experience it—use a "1" if it was very hard to do, a "2" if it was somewhat hard to do, a "3" if it was somewhat easy to do, and a "4" if it was very easy to do.

		Very Hard to Experience 1	Somewhat Hard to Experience 2	Somewhat Easy to Experience 3	Very Easy to Experience 4
1.	Picture the face of the president of the United States.				
2.	Hear yourself singing happy birthday to someone.				
3.	Feel yourself walking rapidly down a set of stairs.				
4.	See the Washington Monument.				
5.	Hear the roar of the crowd at a professional football game.				
6.	Imagine the smell of freshly cut grass.				
7.	Imagine a snow-covered pine tree.				
8.	Listen to a chorus of singers singing God Bless America.				
9.	Taste a fresh peach.				
10.	Visualize a flower garden full of different colored roses.				
11.	Listen to the sound of your footsteps on a loose gravel road.				
12.	Imagine yourself running hard to catch a bus.				

Total your ratings for statement numbers 1, 4, 7, and 10. That total is your visual score. Total your ratings for statement numbers 2, 5, 8, and 11. That total is your verbal (auditory) score. Total your ratings for statement numbers 3, 6, 9, and 12. That total is your kinesthetic score.

Whichever is highest is most likely your preferred mental process. (By the way, the results for this little quiz should be very similar to the results of the self-test a few pages back.) Knowing my preferred process helps me to improve the way I communicate with other people.

For example, if I am a visual person, I probably have a natural tendency to use a lot of visual language like, "That doesn't look good to me," or "Let's see how we can improve it." These statements use visual verbs. If I am talking to an auditory person, I might establish a better connection with that person if I use auditory language—"That doesn't sound right to me" or "Let's talk about how we can improve it." And, if I'm a kinesthetic person, I probably use a lot of words describing my bodily sensations, like "That feels right to me" or "I love the taste of success!"

When Bandler and Grinder were developing the NLP concepts, they interviewed prominent therapists. They found therapists were more successful at establishing rapport with their patients by listening to and matching the mental language of their patients.

It is well known among various professions from therapy to sales that one way of establishing rapport with people is to listen carefully to the language they use as a clue to their preferred mental process and then respond in the same way.

For example, if a person uses visual verbs such as "I see what you're saying," the person is visually processing. Establish rapport by responding with something like, "I'm glad you got the picture."

If a person uses auditory verbs such as "It sounds like you want to go home," the person is auditory. Establish rapport by responding with something like, "You heard it right!"

If a person uses kinesthetic verbs such as "I just can't seem to get a handle on this problem," the person is kinesthetically processing. Establish rapport by responding with something like, "Let me help you get a grip on it."

I practice listening to people to learn which way they are relating to me; by matching them in my responses, I find it easier to communicate and be heard.

When applying these ideas to memory, which modality is better? Well, some researchers have concluded visualizers tend to learn more quickly and be more confident about what they have learned. They are more direct, visualizing the whole of what they are trying to remember, without doing as much piece-by-piece learning as do auditory learners. Sounds good, right?

Well, not so fast, because they also found visualizers tended to get the order of information mixed up more often, changed the information more often, and introduced more new, irrelevant material than did verbal learners. But still, visualizers still remained confident, despite their inaccuracy.

On the other hand, these researchers also discovered verbal learners, compared to visual learners, focused more on major points and names and verbal associations with other things previously learned. It's interesting to note that they did not have as much confidence in how accurate they were, as did visual learners.

It's important to note that it isn't better to be one kind of learner than another. We just have different ways of learning things. If I have reached adulthood favoring one way of learning, there's no reason why I can't develop my skills at the other ways of learning.

Here are a few tips I've learned, using my knowledge of my mental preference to improve my memory, which, remember, is auditory. It's OK to use another modality to support my preferred way of remembering.

For example, if I am trying to remember something verbally or kinesthetically, I create visual images as part of the process, to supplement the verbal and kinesthetic learning. When I am trying to remember a list of items such as phone numbers, I write out the list, look at it, and close my eyes and visualize it. Or when I am introduced to a new person, I visualize him wearing a T-shirt with his name in big red, neon letters across his chest.

When I learn something physical, such as playing golf, I intentionally visualize myself doing it in great detail. I see myself swinging the club. I feel the sensation of the club in my hand. I feel my body as I swing the club to connect with the ball. Researchers have found athletes who couple visualization with actual practice end up performing better than those who simply practice.

Because I favor verbal memory, I use self-talk when I want to remember things. For example, when I meet people, I think their names to myself several times. I can describe them in my head using their names as I do so. In other words, in my thoughts, I talk to myself about them as I meet them.

If my preferred method for remembering is kinesthetic, I attach physical actions to whatever I am trying to remember. If I am meeting new people, for example, I firmly shake their hands as I meet them. I am aware of the touch and pressure of their hands as I shake them. I feel the sound of my voice traveling up and out of me as I say their names.

Of course there's so much more to the concepts of NLP, modality, memory, and accessing cues. Every gesture, twitch of my nose, or rising of my eyebrow is connected to some stored thought or state of mind. There are plenty of resources available to learn more about reading what's on my mind as well as what's on the minds of other people.

For example, *Frogs into Princes* by John Grinder and Richard Bandler, *Total Recall* by Joan Minninger, and *Awaken the Giant Within* by Anthony Robbins are all excellent resources. Another source is AMORC, The Ancient and Mystical Order of Rosae Crucis. These are just a few of the people and resources whose words and wisdom have stimulated my thinking on the topics I've discussed in this chapter.

Concentration—Sister to Memory

Now that you have some rudimentary understanding about NLP and how it relates to memory, I'd like you to try a short but powerful exercise I have found to help me in my quest for a better use of my mind and memory. It's designed to help me to focus and concentrate better. I keep in mind concentration is the sister to memory. I cannot do one effectively without the support of the other. So here's a simple and easy-to-learn technique I use to enhance my power to concentrate.

I do this in the morning when my mind is rested. I could be at my home or sitting at my desk at work. I will do it whenever I have a free minute or two, for that is all the time this exercise takes. I pick out an object. I examine it closely and observe everything about it. I make use of all of my sensors. I notice its size, its color, and its texture.

I pick it up and feel it. I even smell it. I talk to myself about the object. I tell myself about the color and the size, how I see it, how I feel it, and how I touch it. I use all three kinds of memory: visual, auditory, and kinesthetic. I usually take about seventy-five seconds for my observation.

Then I close my eyes and see the object. I visualize every detail. What were its color, its size, and its shape? What was its texture? I remember how it felt to hold it. I recall what I said about it. I recall its smell.

When I am finished, I open my eyes and look at the object again. How clearly was I able to bring the object to mind? Are there some details I missed? Then I close my eyes again and visualize the object once more.

This only takes a minute or two, but when I practice it on a daily basis I find my ability to focus and to concentrate, and yes, to memorize and remember, begins to increase.

Rhyming Number Pegs

Before I move on to the next chapter, I'd like you to try a memory exercise that makes use of all of the modalities you learned about in this chapter—*auditory*, *visual*, and *kinesthetic*. I call this exercise Rhyming Number Pegs.

There are three steps to this exercise. First, you will learn a series of rhyming "number pegs." Second, you will specify the list of items or thoughts you want to remember. Third, you will connect the number pegs to the list.

Rhyming number pegs are a list of words that rhyme with the ten numbers. Rhyming a word with each number is what makes this technique work. My favorite list is one I learned many years ago and still use today:

The rhymes will help you recall the information you associate with each peg.

Now, let's commit these pegs to memory. On the next page, I'm going to verbally create a picture of each of the memory pegs. As you read the description for each of the ten number pegs, read it aloud so you hear it, visualize it as you are reading so you see it, and wherever appropriate, feel the action you are describing, as if you were really doing it.

Here we go.

One is a bun. 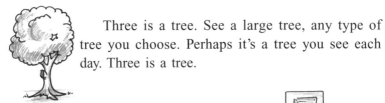 See yourself squeezing the bun, and as you squeeze it, whatever is inside pops out. One is a bun.

Two is a shoe. Make it an extra-large version of a shoe you are familiar with, a shoe you would recognize instantly. Two is a shoe.

Three is a tree. See a large tree, any type of tree you choose. Perhaps it's a tree you see each day. Three is a tree.

Four is a door. See a door that's familiar to you. A door you pass through each day. Four is a door.

Five is a drive. See yourself peering over the steering wheel of your automobile, driving down the road. Five is a drive.

Six is sticks. See two giant drumsticks, one for each hand. Six is sticks.

Seven is heaven.  See an angel sitting on a cloud with large silvery wings and a halo, or whatever represents heaven for you. Seven is heaven.

Eight is a plate. See the dinner plate you use at home, because you are familiar with the color and pattern, which makes it easy to see quickly. Eight is a plate.

Nine is a fishing pole fishing line. See yourself holding a with the line in the water. Nine is a fishing line.

Ten is a pigpen. See a fence around a large puddle of mud in which big pigs are sloshing around. Ten is a pigpen.

Now look again at the list of memory pegs repeated below. Try to see the same pictures you saw as you were reading my descriptions on this and the previous page. Hear yourself reading them. Feel the actions that take place in each picture. OK, here they are.

> One is a bun.
> Two is a shoe.
> Three is a tree.
> Four is a door.
> Five is a drive.
> Six is sticks.
> Seven is heaven.
> Eight is a plate.
> Nine is a fishing line.
> Ten is a pigpen.

Next close this book and write the ten rhyming number pegs on a piece of paper. Then open the book to this page and see if you got them all correct. If not, repeat this process, starting at the top of the last page. Keep doing this until you can correctly write out and speak aloud all ten memory pegs, both in and out of order. At that point, you will have finished step 1.

Ok you're ready for step 2, specifying a list of items or thoughts you want to remember. It could be a list of things you want to do during the day, your daily agenda. Or, it could be a list of items you want to purchase at the store. Or, it could be a list of names. In fact, it could be anything you can make into a list.

For this exercise, I will specify the list. Later on, you can practice with your own lists. Let's use the list below.

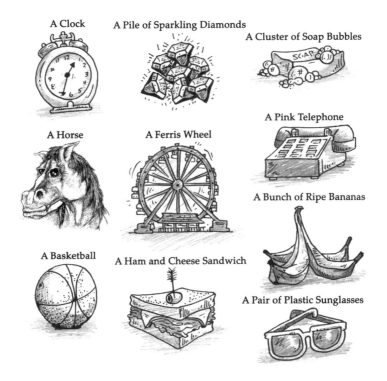

Now we're ready for step 3. Here's where we connect each item on the list to one of the rhyming number pegs we learned on the last few pages. It will help you if you make your connection silly or absurd, so the picture will really stand out in your mind. The more silly or absurd the image, the more likely you'll remember and recall it.

The key here is to go with the first image you see. Don't take time to analyze or perfect your pictures. Analyzing is not necessary for the system to work. In fact, it would probably have the opposite effect. When possible, try to include some motion in your image.

For example, if the first item were an apple, you could have the apple interact in some funny or absurd way with the first rhyming number peg, which of course is a bun. You could see yourself squeezing a hot dog bun full of apples, and watching the apples squish into the air. In other words, recall improves when you get the item or object interacting with the rhyming memory peg.

I'm now going to demonstrate how I would connect the list of items to the memory pegs. Here I go.

The first item on my list is a clock. One is a bun. I visualize myself squeezing a hot dog bun and seeing a clock being squished into the air. A clock is now pegged at number one.

The second item on my list is a horse. Two is a shoe. I see an extra-large shoe tap dancing on the back of a horse. A horse is now pegged at number two.

My third item is a basketball. Three is a tree. I see a basketball dangling on a bungee cord from the branch of a large tree, bouncing up and down—it really helps me when I put some motion into my pictures. A basketball is now pegged at number three.

My fourth item is a pile of sparkling diamonds. Four is a door. I see myself opening a door—as I swing the door open, it knocks over a pile of sparkling diamonds scattering them all over the floor. A pile of sparkling diamonds is now pegged at number four.

The fifth item on my list is a Ferris wheel. Five is a drive. I see myself in my car, going for a drive, and all of a sudden, I crash into a Ferris wheel, which lands with a big plump on the hood of my car. A Ferris wheel is now pegged at number five.

My sixth item is a ham and cheese sandwich. Six is sticks. I see myself using giant turkey drumsticks to beat on a ham and cheese sandwich like a drummer might do, and I watch the ham and cheese squish out from the sides of the sandwich. A ham and cheese sandwich is now pegged at number six.

The seventh item on my list is a cluster of soap bubbles. Seven is heaven. I see an angel sitting on a cloud, blowing a cluster of soap bubbles in the air with a child's bubble pipe, and I see the bubbles floating up and around the angel's head like a soapy halo. A cluster of soap bubbles is now pegged at seven.

My eighth item is a pink telephone. Eight is a plate. I see and feel myself lifting up a plate with a pink telephone on it, which is ringing so loudly I really want to throw the plate and telephone against the wall. A pink telephone is now pegged at eight.

The ninth item on my list is a bunch of ripe bananas. Nine is a fishing line. I see myself snagging my fishing line on a bunch of ripe bananas floating in the water, and I watch them fly up into the air as I pull my fishing line up and back over my head. A bunch of ripe bananas is now pegged at nine.

My tenth item is a pair of plastic sunglasses. Ten is a pigpen. Can't you just see the same big pigs I saw, wearing plastic sunglasses as they slosh around in the mud of a pigpen? A pair of plastic sunglasses is now pegged at ten.

OK, let's see how this registered with you. After you put this book down, write the numbers one through ten down a page, one number per line. Think of the picture you saw with each item and write the item next to the number. After you've finished, check below to see how well you connected the list of information to the rhyming number pegs.

For item one, did you immediately see a clock squishing out of a hot dog bun, into the air?

For item two, did you see an extra-large shoe tap dancing on the back of a horse?

For item three, did you see a basketball dangling from the branch of a large tree, bouncing up and down?

For item four, did you see yourself opening a door, which knocked over a pile of sparkling diamonds, scattering them all over the floor?

For item five, did you see a Ferris wheel plumping on the hood of your car as you drove into it?

For item six, did you see yourself beating on a ham and cheese sandwich with two large turkey drumsticks like a drummer?

For item seven, did you see an angel sitting on a cloud, blowing soap bubbles, which floated up around the angel's head like a halo?

For item eight, did you see yourself lifting up a pink telephone on a plate and wanting to throw the plate and phone against the wall because it was ringing so loudly?

For item nine, did you see yourself yanking a bunch of ripe bananas out of the water as you pulled your fishing line up and back over your head?

For item ten, did you see big pigs, wearing plastic sunglasses and sloshing around in the mud?

Whew! How well did you do? Don't be discouraged if you didn't get them all. With practice, you easily will!

Although it has taken several pages to explain this exercise to you, in reality, you can do it very quickly once you have learned the ten rhyming memory pegs. The pegs give you a valuable tool for remembering all sorts of information.

If you didn't get them all, take a moment to read over the last several pages to learn them, before you read any further. Change any memory peg to anything you prefer, but settle on one set of memory pegs before reading further.

Now you can take it a step further. Believe it or not, once you've mastered this system for remembering, you will be able to recall any of the items on your list, out of order. Try it with the list we just used.

For example, which item is number five? How about number three? How about number seven?

If you carefully worked through this exercise as I was describing it, my guess is you correctly answered all three questions. How about that?

I seldom need to use more than ten memory pegs. However, sometimes, when I'm out to dazzle my friends at a party, I use ten additional pegs—numbers eleven through twenty.

I won't elaborate on each peg as I did with the first ten. I will simply state the number and its rhyming word and give a brief suggested interaction between the peg and how I use it with an item I want to remember.

Incidentally, as with the first ten pegs, create your own pegs if some of these pegs I use don't seem to work for you. My only caution is to make certain to always use the same memory pegs.

Here are the additional pegs:

> **Eleven** is elephant. The elephant is stomping on or about to sit on the item.
> **Twelve** is a shelf. Have the item falling from or bouncing on the shelf.
> **Thirteen** is hurting. Put a large Band-Aid on the object.
> **Fourteen** is courting. Put item between two lover's lips.
> **Fifteen** is lifting. The item is lifted with one finger.
> **Sixteen** is fixing. Repair the item in some unusual way.
> **Seventeen** isn't seen. Place the item under a microscope.
> **Eighteen** is eating. A shark is eating the item.
> **Nineteen** is lightning. The lightning is striking the item.
> **Twenty** is a horn of plenty. Place the item prominently into the horn of plenty.

And there they are, along with the first ten, a structure of twenty rhyming memory pegs. Twenty mental images I use to memorize bits of information.

I mentioned using the extra ten at a party. But I find the most practical use for a memory technique such as this one is to fix in my mind the random thoughts that flit through it at precisely the times when I can't possibly write them down or act on them. For instance, when I'm driving, or when I'm in the shower, or when I'm drifting off to sleep, or when I'm "paying attention" to a business associate, a relative, or a friend.

I use this rhyming number peg system whenever an idea comes to me while I am totally involved in something else.

By the way, if what I want to remember is an abstraction, I try to make it into a solid image, a face, an object, or a symbol. Then, instead of reaching for a pencil, I reach for a peg—a rhyming number peg—designed to record my thought until I can play it back at a more convenient time.

Naturally, I don't claim ownership of this mnemonic system. After all, it's been around for thousands of years. Mnemosyne was the Greek goddess of memory. She was the mother of the muses. Her namesake, "mnemonics," simply means memory aids. A mnemonic can be simple or complex, sensible or foolish.

One final note before I leave this exercise. Remember to use all three modalities as you learn the memory peg system: visual, auditory, and kinesthetic—see, hear, and touch and feel the scenarios you create. The more you involve all three modalities, and the sillier, more absurd are your pictures, the better this technique will work for you.

It's All about Choice

I believe I was born with perfect memory abilities. The question is what are my memory habits? What can I do to improve upon what has served me so well all of these many years?

Anyone who chooses to can redevelop his or her memory habits at any point in his or her life. Many people don't realize it's all about choice. They accept what they believe about themselves without even thinking.

I will get more into this subject in the next chapter.

Meanwhile, I don't want you to think I'm straying from my intention to teach you how to read minds. Remember, I am using memory as a tool to help you do that. And, in the next several chapters, I will provide you with more tools—many of them focused around memory exercises.

And, yes, I will get to mind reading later in the book. First, let's continue to build our foundation.

CHAPTER SIX

Beliefs: I Do What I Believe I Can Do

One person with a belief is equal to a force of ninety-nine who have only interests.
—*John Stuart Mill (1806-1873)*
British philosopher and writer

Now I come to a very important obstacle to effective memory that has to do with my belief system. Becoming aware of this obstacle and doing something about it helps me to improve my memory. But more than that, it points the way to many areas of self-discovery and opens the door to the possibility of mind reading.

My Beliefs and My Self-Talk

Recall my discussion of "self-talk" when I was covering the basics of NLP (Neuro-Linguistic Programming). We are all constantly engaged in self-talk. Whether I am listening to someone speak, listening to a radio, watching and listening to something on television, or just sitting and doing nothing, I am continuously talking to myself in my mind—I am engaged in self-talk all of my waking day.

And much of that self-talk is focused on beliefs about myself, about other people, about the nature of things that happen in the world around me.

Those beliefs lead me to make a lot of assumptions about my world—about the way it works, about people, about myself, about what I can and cannot do. These assumptions influence the choices I make and therefore the actions I take or do not take.

Consider an example directly related to memory. Suppose I was one of those people who say, "I just can't remember names!" That statement would be a direct reflection of my self-talk—my internal belief I just cannot ever remember names. If I go around telling myself I can't remember names, chances are I never will be able to remember names! Without realizing it, I will have limited my ability.

Sociologists call this "self-fulfilling prophecy," which means as I believe it to be, so shall it become. When I believe I will never be able to do something (prophecy), I become incapable of doing it (self-fulfilling).

The other side of the coin, of course, is if I believe I *will* be able to do something, chances are I will find a way to do it—the self-fulfilling prophecy! That's why so many books and articles on the power of positive thinking are so popular—they help people to achieve powerful shifts in their thinking and therefore their actions or behaviors they might not otherwise achieve. My beliefs become self-fulfilling. However, I've concluded that no amount of *positive thinking* alone will ever help me to achieve anything without fueling my thoughts with *positive action!*

Caught in the Classic Vicious Belief Cycle

Do I believe I can change a longtime belief/habit/addiction? If I think "yes," then I am already free from a barrier that stops many people from changing. If I think "no," then I may not realize that I, and no one else, stopped me from developing my ability to make a choice to change.

Once again, the power of negative beliefs rears its unwelcome head. When I believe I really don't have the capacity to change, I will fail every time I try to change—remember the "self-fulfilling prophecy"?

Here's how it goes. I make a few tentative attempts at changing a habit, and at the first sign of failure—the first time I can't accomplish my goal—I say to myself, "I just don't do very well at this kind of thing." Then I reason: "It must be because I'm not able to change." And what does that leave me with? A belief: "I cannot change."

What I've done is trap myself in a vicious belief cycle. My belief that I am not creative influences my perception—my interpretation—of how well I do when I try to be creative.

I failed. I then do what we all learned to do when we were little tots. I ask "Why?" I come up with an explanation: "It must be because I'm not creative." That's where it becomes vicious. My explanation further reinforces the very belief I started with!

My Positive and Negative Beliefs

It is important for me to understand that as an adult, I am already programmed with many sets of positive and negative beliefs. Each belief, whether positive or negative, will produce a result along with its own assortment of consequences.

My battle to stop smoking is a perfect example of how my (silent but negative) belief about changing a habit resulted in a lengthy and painful struggle. I began smoking one or two cigarettes a week when I was eleven years old. By the time I was twenty-six I was smoking up to five packs a day. I finally decided I had enough of the coughing and the odor in my home, my car, my clothes, and in my hair. I began to consider quitting. And so I began the cycle of making a New Year's resolution I would quit smoking. I did this, to no avail, each year for the next four years. And each year, the commitment to quit became more difficult.

Although I did not know it at the time the reason it became more difficult was that I was actually fighting two battles. The first battle was the fact that smoking is both a physical addiction and a mental habit. The second battle was the contempt I felt for myself for failing to meet my commitment.

This mental attitude developed into a *belief*, an *assumption* that I would fail, I could not succeed. And each year, after I made my New Year's resolution and was unable to quit, it became harder for me to do so the next year. My belief that I could not achieve my goal was reinforced by the negative assumption that since I could not accomplish this effort in the past, I would not be able to accomplish it in the future.

I was finally motivated by my five-year-old daughter, Laurie Beth, who, having seen the "Kick The Habit" TV ad aimed at asking people to quit smoking, asked me to *Kick The Habit*. She wanted to be sure I would be around when she was older to tell her she was beautiful and I loved her. That same winter I participated in a workshop named the Five-Day Plan. The workshop was conducted by a family physician along with a minister with the Seventh-Day Adventist Church. Armed with the information and direction I learned in this workshop, I was able to stop smoking.

This experience led me to radically shift my thinking. First, I changed my belief (negative fulfilling prophecy) I would fail to my new belief (positive fulfilling prophecy) I can and will succeed. Second, I shifted my assumption I could not change my longtime habit to the assumption I could change. Third, I changed my self-talk from "I must quit" to "I choose not to smoke." It worked! To this day, I choose not to smoke. So my reality is that I am in the habit of not smoking. This is a perfect example of changing my perception and turning it into a new reality.

The Power of My Assumptions

Here is a perfect example of the amazing power of holding onto an ongoing assumption. Especially one that is false. I was taught in elementary school that in 1492 Christopher Columbus and his small fleet consisting of the *Niña*, the *Pinta*, and the *Santa Maria* left the port of Palos, Spain, where they had been fitted out, and headed for the Canary Islands, where they would pick up northeast trade winds. Six weeks later they would leave the Canaries, and three months later they would bump into the Americas.

The story purported that in his day, sailors believed that the world was flat. So, whenever they traveled out from land for several days they would become nervous because they didn't want to go too far and sail off the ends of the earth.

The farther they traveled, the more nervous they became. As the days passed and the distance traveled grew and grew, the nervousness often began to turn into panic—*"We don't want to sail off the edge of the earth!"*

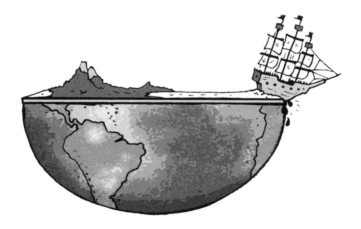

In some instances the sailors became so panicked they mutinied against the captain, took over the ship, and sailed back to land. That's a very powerful connection between an assumption and behavior!

But there's more to this story than I knew. See, up until this time I assumed the "flat earth" story was true. After all, I learned it in school—why wouldn't it be true?

However, a dear friend and colleague, Marcello Truzzi, alerted me to the fact that this was a myth and suggested I do some research on the topic. Marcello passed away about a week after he made this and other suggestions to me about specific information I was including in this book. He will live eternally in my heart and mind, and he will be remembered by many of his friends and family as a true scholar and as a man filled with curiosity and the will to search out the veracity of both sides to a specific claim.

My search for the truth about this myth was easily answered by doing a search on the internet. According to Jeffrey Burton Russell, author of the book, *The Myth of the Flat Earth*, along with a summary he delivered for the American Scientific Affiliation Conference, the story of Columbus and his search for the answer to the notion that the earth was flat is not at all true. It seems the story was the fictional invention of none other than the well-known author of such works as *The Legend of Sleepy Hollow* and *Rip Van Winkle*—Washington Irving.

In 1828, Irving wrote a best-seller about Columbus. He described a dramatic confrontation where Columbus had to win over disbelieving scholars.

Actually, Aristotle proved the earth was round two thousand years earlier, pointing out the curved shadow it casts on the moon. By Columbus's time, people took it for granted.

The real argument was over the size of the ocean—and Columbus was wrong, because he thought it was a short sail to India.

But Irving's version made Columbus the hero . . . and myth became enshrined as history.

Yet another example of the power of belief and assumption is what some eighteenth-century physicians believed about people who were nasty and behaved badly. They believed it was because these people had evil spirits in them. So what was the cure? Simple. Drill a hole in their head to let the evil spirits out! I can't think of a better historical example of the power of assumptions in influencing behavior.

Testing Assumptions

Here is an exercise you can use to demonstrate the role assumptions play in your own life. It's been around for years. Even if you've tried it before, try it again—you may be in for a surprise. I have provided four copies of the diagram below on the next page. If your belief is that you prefer not to write on the pages of this book then get a sheet of paper and a pencil and duplicate the image below. You may find that you will need several tries to solve this puzzle.

Along the top of the paper, draw three round dots, as shown above. Similarly, draw three dots in the middle, and at the bottom.

Next, connect all nine dots with one continuous straight line that changes direction no more than twice. For example:

BELIEFS: I DO WHAT I BELIEVE I CAN DO

Were you able to do it? If not, you are being stopped from doing so by an assumption you are making—an assumption you learned to make before you even started school. The solution is revealed on the next page.

If you were not able to figure out how to connect all nine dots with one continuous straight line that changes directions no more than two times, you were probably trapped by the following assumption: "I must stay on the page." Remember Mom saying, "Color between the lines" and later, some teacher grading you for neatness with your homework. Given all of those old messages, you certainly wouldn't consider going off the edge of the page!

It's easy to do if you draw lines that extend off the page as I've done in the diagram below.

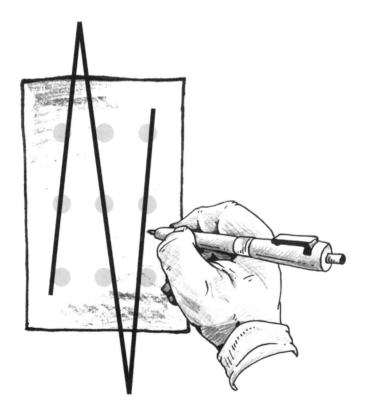

This exercise very nicely illustrates how assumptions I make, without even realizing I've made them, can affect my ability to do something.

But I'm not just stopping there! You probably don't realize it, but you were making several other assumptions about the exercise when you were attempting to connect the dots. Let's uncover those assumptions by modifying the exercise.

Take a fresh sheet of paper and once again draw nine dots on the paper in positions just like you did for the previous exercise:

This time, I invite you to connect all nine dots *with one continuous straight line that **does not turn at all**,* as illustrated below:

Try to connect the circles with one straight line *before* you read any further. If you think you have the solution or just plain give up, now is the time to turn the page.

In fact there are several solutions to this problem. Consider some other assumptions you may have made. "I can't cut the page." "I must use a standard-sized pencil." "I can't move or fold the page."

Let's take the first assumption: "I can't cut the page." Sure you can. I didn't say anything about not cutting the page when I gave you the instructions! You could cut each circle out, line them all up, and draw a straight line through them like so:

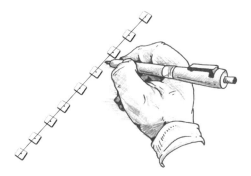

Or you could take the nine circles, stack them up, and push the point of your pencil through them like this. How about another assumption you probably made: "I can't move or fold the page." *Who* told you that?

You could fold the page in such a way that the circles overlap each other and then, using a wide pencil, draw a line through all nine of them like so. Have I made my point?

The assumptions I make can be very powerful blocks to accomplishing my goals and to achieving the desired results as I look for solutions to life's many challenges.

The Filter of My Beliefs and My Assumptions

Clearly, my beliefs and assumptions act as a filter, influencing what I hear, what I see, and what I do.

Consider the following diagram as it relates to my ability to perceive, to listen, and to be consciously creative.

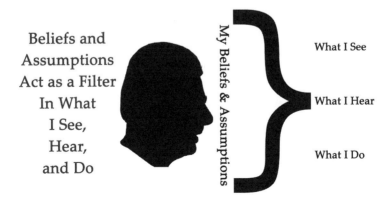

Becoming aware of how my beliefs filter interpretations of my experiences as those experiences become registered in my brain is an important step to improving any of my mental skills. The use of my memory is a perfect example of the role my beliefs and assumptions play as I am unconsciously filtering my interpretations.

When I *believe* I can improve my memory, I have taken the first and most important step in doing so. This means first identifying those thoughts that surround my self-defeating beliefs, then challenging them.

Let's say my belief is that I will never be able to improve my memory. Following are some examples of surrounding thoughts and challenges to them.

Surrounding thought: "I've never been able to remember names!" *Challenge*: "That was then and this is now. With the proper training and exercise of discipline, I *will* be able to improve my memory."

Surrounding thought: "No matter how hard I've tried, I've never been able to remember phone numbers!" *Challenge*: "Given the way I do it now, it isn't working. But there must be other techniques I can learn that *will* work. I will discover those techniques and try them."

Surrounding thought: "I'm getting older, and I know memory fades as a person ages." *Challenge*: "That's just an excuse. Contemporary brain research supports the notion that I have to use it or lose it! I may drop a few brain cells as I get older, but I sure can improve my memory by stimulating the cells I have!"

The nice thing about this approach—identifying the thoughts surrounding my beliefs and challenging them—is it isn't limited to my belief about my ability to remember. It applies to any self-defeating belief I might have.

By the way, I'm *not saying* I can absolutely do anything. After all, if I were four feet one inch tall, I probably wouldn't have much of a chance to become another Michael Jordan!

What I *am saying* is many of my beliefs stifle me in far more situations than I previously may have realized.

Particularly important to improving my memory is training myself to be aware of how my beliefs and assumptions distort what I see and hear. For example, if I am a passionate Democrat, I probably will see a conservative Republican as someone who is not credible. As a result, I will not pay much attention to him or her, or I will only selectively hear what he or she has to say, or I will not store what he or she has to say, because it won't fit my mental model. Any of these actions work against my having an effective memory.

Of course, I do not have to give up all of my beliefs and assumptions. In fact, beliefs and assumptions help me make sense of my world. However, I must constantly challenge those beliefs and assumptions. I need to constantly expand my mind, or at least make myself aware of how my beliefs and assumptions will limit or outright distort the information that gets into my brain.

The Importance of My Choices

The other concept besides *belief* that emerges as a cornerstone of the past several chapters is the concept of *choice*.

Every action I take is a choice. Even in situations where I think I have no choice, I do, in fact, have a choice. Consider as an example the following conversation:

"I have to go to work."

"Why do I have to go to work?"

"I need to earn money."

"Why do I need to earn money?"

"I need money to live! I need money to buy food to feed myself. I need money to clothe myself. I need money to keep a roof over my head, to buy a car, to go to lunch, and all kinds of other things that will make my life safe and pleasurable."

"So, if I don't go to work, I won't earn money; then I won't be able to feed, clothe, house, and pleasure myself, right?"

"Right."

"I still don't *have* to go to work."

"What do I mean?"

"I could decide I don't need all of those things to live and not go to work. The fact is, I *choose* to go to work, because if I don't, I won't earn the money I need to feed, clothe, house, and pleasure myself. The point is I go to work, because *I choose* to go to work!"

When I stop to think about it, I literally make thousands of choices every day of my life. I know every step I take, every turn of my head, every word I speak, every action I take—all of these are choices!

Now here's where my beliefs and my assumptions come back into the picture. They *structure* the window through which I see my world. If I believe I am not capable of doing something, then I won't choose to take actions that would lead me to do it. If, as in the earlier Democrat-Republican example, my political beliefs lead me to strongly reject an opponent's argument, I will choose to reject his credibility. Furthermore, I may choose to not even listen to him or her!

To sharpen my mental abilities, to expand my mind, to increase my flexibility and adaptability, all of which greatly help me in my quest to improve my memory, I need to build many more windows in my personal house!

Somebody told me a story recently they had read about a young child in school that went something like this. The teacher asked everyone to color a drawing of a scene in which there were trees, grass, and the sky. All of the little tots conscientiously colored the sky blue and the trees and grass a bright green.

All, that is, except for one child who colored the sky a deep purple and lavender and the trees and grass almost black. The teacher put a big *X* through the drawing. The child was perplexed and complained to the teacher.

The teacher asked the child why he colored the sky a deep purple and lavender and the trees and grass almost black. The child said, "Because that's the way it looks to me when I wake up in the morning just before I can see the sun come up!"

The teacher's "blue" and "green" assumptions trapped her into not even seeing another possibility. To make matters worse, her action confused the child and maybe put a damper on his creativity skill.

I walk around every day making choices generated by my beliefs and my assumptions about which I am not at all conscious. They reside in what some people call my unconscious mind. At some time in my life they were conscious—something a parent said, something a teacher said, something I read, and so on. But after I accepted them and moved on to other experiences, those beliefs and assumptions faded back into my unconscious mind.

My mind contains a large number of such unconscious beliefs and assumptions that affect the choices I make. In order to expand my mind and enlarge my window to the world, I need to uncover them so I can decide whether or not they are worth holding anymore.

"But how can I do that?" "How can I look at something that's invisible, because it's in my unconscious mind?"

Simple. The door to my beliefs and my assumptions is the choice I make at any given moment. When I make a choice, I ask myself why and why again until a belief or assumption pops to the surface. Then I can decide whether that belief or assumption still serves me well. I then can make a *conscious* choice.

This is where the I/You Concept works so well for me. When I consciously choose to use "I" instead of "you," I think about my underlying belief or assumption and I question whether it is still valid for me.

My Level of Comfort and My Risk-Taking

There are a couple of more factors at work here: my level of comfort in a situation and the extent to which I am willing to take a risk.

Many people find it difficult to behave in ways they normally do not. Some psychologists refer to this as my "comfort zone." I am so used to behaving the way I behave it's stressful to do something different. In some cases it may be a simple behavior that causes me to feel uneasy. In others, it may be downright risky.

Consider, for example an exercise trainers use in workshop settings. If I normally wear my watch on my left wrist, the trainer tells me to take it off and wear it for a while on my right wrist. This doesn't exactly ruin my day, but it does feel a little strange for at least a while. Try it for a day!

Take this a step further. If I am a person who wears a watch all day, every day, the trainer tells me to take it off for a couple of days and walk around without it. This feels a little more than strange—I feel "lost" without it for a while when I first try it.

These are simple examples that don't involve much risk. Now I want to consider some examples that are a little more risky.

In our society, most of us prepare ourselves to go out in public. We comb our hair and dress "appropriately" before we step outside. Try an experiment. Get up one morning, don't bother to comb your hair (in fact, mess it up a little), dress in some ratty old clothes, put on mismatched socks (or none at all), and then go out to a business meeting.

Whew! When I first tried that, it was really difficult to do. I was way out of my comfort zone. I felt extremely stressed. Why? Because I was worried about how other people were looking at me. What they were thinking about me. How they were evaluating me. Why? Because I believed there were certain proper ways of dressing and appearing at a meeting or in public.

I believed I would be judged as dumb or crazy or rude or insensitive or some such thing.

I'm right back to beliefs and assumptions again.

Even some simple beliefs, like this one about my appearance are uncomfortable to challenge.

By the way, I'm not trying to get anyone to change such a belief about his or her appearance. I was simply using this as an example of how risky it can be to challenge what most people wouldn't rank among their most important of beliefs.

There are some other beliefs that are far more important to people and far more risky to challenge. Take beliefs about failure, for example. Many people do everything they can to avoid failure. Why? Look at some of the beliefs surrounding failure. I will be seen as "less than." People will look at me as dumb. It is not good to fail. People won't respect me if I fail. I won't make any progress if I fail. These are all great big tension producers, making it very risky to fail.

So what do these people do? They make choices to do things in ways they know won't result in failure. This means they are excluding all kinds of choices that might give them new insights, new information, and new "windows" for looking at the world.

Here's where a technique I'll discuss in chapter 10 comes in handy: *reframing*. Instead of viewing failure as bad, look at it as an opportunity to learn.

Look at it as an opportunity to grow. That's what successful people do. Instead of looking at the 1,800 light bulbs made by Edison as failures, look at them the way Edison did. He viewed them as 1,800 ways *not* to make a light bulb. He learned from all of them. You know the rest of the story.

My Beliefs and My Memory

Now I want to come back to memory—particularly my skill at remembering names. What should I do if I believe (make the assumption) I just can't ever remember names?

The first step is for me to challenge that belief, that self-talk, *every time* it happens. I must challenge such a belief every time by saying to myself something like: "Wait a minute! I *can* remember names of people—I just have to figure out how to do it. I have to come up with some techniques, some actions I can take to help me succeed at it!" The trick is to *consistently* challenge myself *every time* I catch myself in any kind of self-defeating, I-can't-do-it kind of self-talk.

The next step, now that I am telling myself I *can* remember names, is to come up with some techniques that will help me do so. What I need is an exercise I can practice doing over and over again until remembering names becomes easy.

Remember my discussion of NLP? Recall that I connect my visual, auditory, and kinesthetic sensory experiences to my thinking, and this leads me to three principal kinds of memory: *visual, verbal,* and *kinesthetic.*

In light of this knowledge, it's reasonable to assume that an exercise using all three kinds of memory would be the most effective way to sharpen my skill at remembering names.

My Three-Minute Exercise for Remembering Names

Here's an exercise that I call *Take Three,* because it's an exercise I can repeat three times in three minutes. It will teach me to use all three types of memory in a systematic way, every time I use it. The steps for this exercise are shown in the chart on the next page:

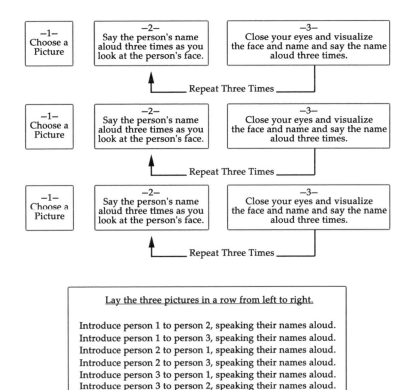

The object of this exercise is to get in the habit of connecting names to faces on a regular basis. If it is practiced consistently, along with an exercise I will present on a later page, there will be an amazing transformation at how quickly the skill of remembering names (and faces) will improve.

Learning anything new takes time. And it takes disciplined consistency. Do this exercise three days a week, at the same time every day, for a period of three weeks. Pick the most alert time—for some people it's early morning; for others it's later in the day. Do it before eating or after a period of rest.

Here's how it goes. Go through a newspaper or a magazine or any other publication that has pictures of people accompanied by their names—people whom you do not know. Cut out the three pictures and separately cut out their names. As an alternative, print their names on separate slips of paper. Then follow the steps of introducing one person to another as indicated in the charts on the previous page.

For now, though, let's use the photos of three pharmaceutical representatives who have so generously allowed me to use their names and photographs for this exercise.

This lovely lady's name is

Becki Anderson

1. Say **Becki Anderson** aloud three times as you look at her face.
2. Close your eyes and visualize Becki Anderson's face and name and say **Becki Anderson** aloud three times.
3. Repeat steps 1 and 2 three times.

The name of the pleasant gentleman in this photograph is

Raymond Rodriguez

1. Say **Raymond Rodriguez** aloud three times as you look at his face.
2. Close your eyes and visualize Raymond Rodriguez's face and name and say **Raymond Rodriguez** aloud three times.
3. Repeat steps 1 and 2 three times.

BELIEFS: I DO WHAT I BELIEVE I CAN DO

This cheerful lady's name is

Meg Marian

1. Say **Meg Marian** aloud three times as you look at her face.
2. Close your eyes and visualize Meg Marian's face and name and say **Meg Marian** aloud three times.
3. Repeat steps 1 and 2 three times.

So far, you've used your visual and auditory senses. We will now add the kinesthetic sense with the last step in this exercise shown in the flowchart back on page 101.

First we arrange all three pictures in a row (kinesthetic) with their names:

Becki Anderson   **Raymond Rodriguez**   **Meg Marian**

Then we systematically introduce each person to each of the others, saying their names aloud as we do so:

> Becki Anderson, I'd like you to meet Raymond Rodriguez.
> Becki Anderson, I'd like you to meet Meg Marian.
> Raymond Rodriguez, I'd like you to meet Becki Anderson.
> Raymond Rodriguez, I'd like you to meet Meg Marian.
> Meg Marian, I'd like you to meet Becki Anderson.
> Meg Marian, I'd like you to meet Raymond Rodriguez.

When you repeat this exercise using photos you cut out of a newspaper or magazine, you can make your experience even more kinesthetic than just arranging them in a row. You might pick up the first picture in each pair with your left hand and introduce him to the second picture in the pair, which you've picked up in your right hand.

This exercise may seem complicated at first, but with a couple of runs through it, you will discover it is actually quite simple.

Discipline yourself to do this exercise with different pictures three times every day for three days.

During the three days, there are several other things you can do to reinforce your new skill. For example, throughout the course of a day, as I interact with people, I use their names in conversation as much as I naturally can. When I am introduced to people, I say their names aloud while looking directly at them: "Pleased to meet you, Becki Anderson." I find ways to use their names several times as I talk to them or when I talk about them to someone else.

Pop the Balloon!

Memory experts have come up with several other things I can do to improve my skills at remembering names.

For instance, here's another simple exercise I use for remembering names. Try using it whenever you meet someone. Most of us meet people during the course of our work each day, but if you don't, then go out of your way to ask people their names—for example, the checkout person at the grocery store or a salesperson or a potential new friend. During the three weeks you are practicing the first exercise, make it a point to do this second exercise at least once a day (more if you have the opportunity).

In this exercise, I create pictures and link them to people's names. There are two simple steps to this process for remembering names. Step 1 is to be certain the information enters my mind in the first place. Step 2 requires me to use my natural ability to instantly create mental pictures. I use the acronym AIR to help me remember people's names.

I will start with the basis for the pictures I create. I close my eyes and visualize a large yellow balloon. I see myself with a pin in my hand. Then I see myself popping the balloon with the pin. As I pop the balloon, I see three large red letters of the alphabet—**A**, **I**, and **R**—escaping from the shriveling balloon, one at a time, watching each letter as it escapes. When all three have escaped, I see them become attached to each other to form the acronym **AIR**.

The acronym **AIR** now becomes a trigger word for me to recall this exercise.

A stands for attention. It is most important to pay attention when I first hear someone's name. And for many of us, this is the most difficult thing to do. Why? Because of the self-talk I mentioned earlier. Suppose I am a doctor, for example. I've just finished working with a patient. I'm transcribing or writing down my notes. I'm starting to walk by a sales representative. I stop and chat for a moment. I talk to a nurse. Then I look at the chart for the next patient. I'm busy, busy, busy. It's all I can do to pay attention. Add to that, I am constantly assessing, judging, and evaluating the situation. I am always having an internal conversation with myself. I'm looking at people's clothing, their jewelry, or the expression on a person's face. I may mentally note how much this person looks like my uncle Harry (and I didn't like Uncle Harry). When I meet someone, there is a distinct possibility I am listening to myself, rather than to the person who is speaking the name!

However, I make a conscious choice to turn away from my present thoughts and pay close attention to listening and absorbing the person's name. Believe me, this does take practice. But, as with all habits, I can make the shift over time.

I stands for interest. I am interested in a person from the moment I see him. I am impressed with the person before I hear his or her name. I use the first three seconds of my encounter to notice the person's characteristics. I pick something that appeals to me. I look at him or her with the eyes of a child. I find I cannot forget someone I am *interested* in. It is imperative I pay attention to that person's agenda rather than my own. It also helps me if I can accept and love that person. Could I possibly forget someone I love?

R is for repeat. I repeat the person's name at the end of my conversation or ask the person to repeat it or even to spell the last name. I consciously listen as the person says or spells it! I will usually see a smile on the person's face, because asking people about their names tells them I am truly interested in them. It's a signal that I want to remember them. I like them.

It is in this moment, when I repeat the person's name at the end of this **AIR** conversation, I create a silly picture that represents their name.

As I say or hear their name, I quickly create a silly or ridiculous picture for the last name—the more ridiculous the better! I'm never concerned with the logic of my image. I just allow it to happen. I make sure to insert the first name into my image as well. If I have a mental reference for the person's name, I will distort it, exaggerate it, or embellish on it. For instance, say the name I want to store away was "Tom Dooley." I already have a reference in my mind for that name. Since I'm an auditory thinker I automatically think of the verse in the song—"hang down your head Tom Dooley . . ."

But now, what about those names for which I do not have a reference? Well then what I do is create pictures out of the syllables or "sound-alike" words of a person's name. I will be providing you with examples of this in just a moment.

Once I have created my picture for the person's name I want to link or associate it. By this, I mean I want to mentally have my picture interact, in a bizarre, absurd, or funny way, with some part of the person's head or face.

Using my example above for the name "Tom Dooley" it would be easy for me to see this person with a tree and a noose growing out of his forehead. Also, I could hear and see hands playing the sound of tom-tom drums on his head to trigger his first name.

AIR: Attention, Interest, and Repeat

I'm now going to present an example of how to go about creating silly pictures out of people's names. Keep in mind, although my description of this process may have seemed lengthy, it actually takes about five to ten seconds to do.

To begin, I use the last name to create an idea or scene. I then insert the first name into that image. If that doesn't immediately cause me to see a starting scene, I switch to the first name and give it a try. Using this approach, I usually find myself easily coming up with an interesting picture that will trigger someone's name.

Also, I develop my picture from left to right or from top to bottom to give me a starting place from which to work.

To demonstrate this process, I've received permission to use the names and pictures of three more pharmaceutical representatives who participated in one of my client's exhibits at medical conferences. Their names are Mary Beth MaGuire, Orest Zbyr and Tanya Bakenhester.

Mary Beth MaGuire

It was easy to quickly think of an existing reference for the name MaGuire. My reference, of course, is Mark McGuire, the home run hitter. His name is spelled differently (McGuire), but it sounds the same, and so it can act as a sound-alike reference. In my mental picture I see Mark McGuire standing to the right of Mary Beth's head. He is wearing a Cardinal baseball cap and has a bat in his hands.

Of course I want to remember Mary Beth and not Mark so I see Mark wearing a wedding gown. Why? Because he is getting "Mary"ed. Where? In a "Beth-tub." OK, now it's your turn. Say the name Mary Beth MaGuire just one time as you look at her image and think of the silly picture I described. Always make the connection absurd or ridiculous and give it some kinesthetic support, some motion or activity. I will talk more about kinesthetic support a little later. I see him gently tapping Mary Beth's eyes with his bat. This image allows me to link my silly picture to her face so the next time I see her face it will trigger the name MaGuire.

Now make sure to say the name Mary Beth MaGuire as you think about that picture I have just described and link it to her face.

Next, we see a photo of a distinguished-looking man with an unusual name.

Orest Zbyr

So unusual I do not have an immediate reference for his first or last name. No problem because I can create a reference from a word that sounds like Orest. That word is "forest." I notice Orest has a lot of forehead so I see a forest of trees sprouting from his forehead. Every tree has a carving on it of the letter *f* inside the international symbol for *no*, which is a circle with a slash across its diameter. Take away the *f*, and I have Orest. For his last name

Zbyr I see a bottle of beer scooting up and down Orest's nose. There is a large *Z* on the beer. OK, say the name Orest Zbyr as you think of this absurd picture representing his name.

Here is our last photograph. It is of a caring woman whose name is:

Tanya Bakenhester

Don't become nervous. This will be very easy to do.

When I first met Tanya, she told me she would allow me to use her name but I must pronounce it correctly. It's Tan-yah not Tahn-ya. Well, as soon as she said that I had my reference.

I saw the ice skater named Tanya, twirling around on the top of her head. And every time her face twirled around I saw a very *tan Tan-yah*.

For Bakenhester I simply split her name into two parts. "Baken" and "hester." I saw Tanya bend over and put some bacon into the oven. She is wearing a jester costume. But since I want to recall "hester" and not "jester" I see a big letter *H* on her outfit.

OK, now say the name Tanya Bakenhester as you think of that silly picture.

Once again this exercise sounds quite involved and complicated, but once you start using it regularly, you will find it to be so simple to do.

Homework—Practice Makes Perfect!

Here's some homework for you. Each day, when you read a name in the paper or hear a name spoken aloud, take a brief moment to translate it into an absurd picture. You'll soon become proficient, and then you'll be ready to try the next step with people you meet. Which is to quickly create your silly or absurd picture and then to place the picture somewhere on the person's face.

After some practice, I find I don't even have to see the person to recall his or her name. The mere fact I am taking the time to focus on his or her name is a great step towards remembering it.

Try this simple system for remembering and recalling names. It does work. With some practice you'll be looking forward to meeting new people, and what a delight it will be to use their names during your encounter and to call them by name the next time you see them.

OK, let's see if you can recall the names of the three sales representatives. Write their names beneath their photographs.

_____   _____   _____

Before I end this chapter, I don't want to forget where it began—talking about how my beliefs become assumptions (self-talk) which limit my actions.

It isn't just my ability to remember things that's affected by my self-talk. All of my behavior—how I define myself, how I interact with others, the goals I set, what I accomplish—are all affected by what I assume. I will get to those topics in a later chapter.

But first, I want to consider how my self-talk affects the way I perceive people and things around me. My perceptions play an important role in my ability to remember—and to read minds.

CHAPTER SEVEN

Perception: I See What I Think I See

> Every man feels that perception gives him an invincible belief of the existence of that which he perceives; and that this belief is not the effect of reasoning, but the immediate consequence of perception.
> —*Thomas Reid (1710-1796)*
> *Scottish philosopher*

Social psychologists have concluded that when someone is trying to persuade us, we are especially influenced if we see that person as an expert, as trustworthy, and as having good intentions. They refer to such a person as a highly credible communicator.

They go on to say that if the very same message is presented in two situations—one in which the communicator is viewed as highly credible and the other in which the communicator is seen as having no credibility—only the highly credible communicator will be influential.

I've thought much about what this means.

To start with, I once again see the power of beliefs in action. If I believe someone is credible, I will be more influenced by that person.

But wait. Something important is happening in between my belief and being influenced.

If I believe someone is credible, then I will see that person as credible. I will look at that person with respect, maybe even admiration. My perception is affected by what I believe!

In another study conducted years ago, researchers studied the owners of Volkswagen cars. They found that those owners who were proud to own a Volkswagen saw it as smaller than those who were indifferent about their car.

In still another study, children who drew pictures of Santa Claus drew them larger before Christmas than they did when they drew them after Christmas.

Back to the Power of My Assumptions

In the last chapter, I talked about the power of my assumptions in determining my behavior. Similarly, the assumptions I make influence what I see.

For example, consider this illustration.

If I assume the background of this drawing is white, I see two faces looking at each other. On the other hand, if I assume the background of this drawing is black, I see a white pedestal or vase in the center of the drawing.

My Perception and Its Context

When I am looking at something, the context in which it is embedded influences what I perceive.

Here's a very simple example of how context influences perception. Look at the two vertical lines below. "Which line is longer, **A** or **B**?

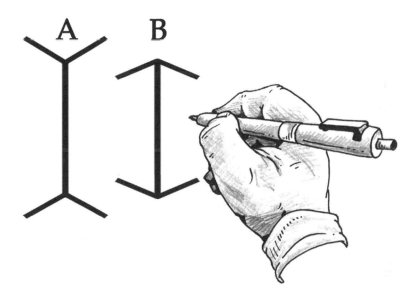

Most people who see this for the first time say **A** is longer. I know when I first saw these two lines next to each other, I immediately saw the line on the left as longer!

But wait a minute! Is it really? Turn the page and see a different perception.

When I draw a horizontal line at the tips of the arrowheads, I see that the vertical lines are of the same length!

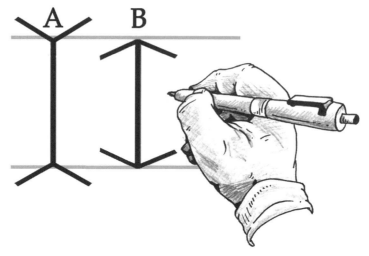

The arrow-like ends of each line create the context, and we end up seeing something that is not so.

Here's another example of context, a little more complicated than the two lines. When I look at the gray figure embedded in a group of antelopes, I will see the figure as an antelope.

But if I see the same gray figure embedded in a group of birds, I will see the figure as a bird.

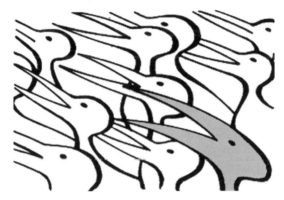

Context Affects My Behavior

An interesting study performed in the late 1980s illustrates both the power of context and its effect on our behavior. A researcher asked one group to find names of people in a matrix containing a variety of letters. The letters were associated with people who are generally classified as hostile—Charlie Manson, Adolph Hitler, and Dracula.

A second group performed the same task, but their matrix of letters contained the hidden names of people generally classified as gentle—Peter Pan, the Pope, Shirley Temple, and good old Santa Claus. Both groups were then exposed to an ambiguous description of a person named "Donald." Everyone was then asked to rate Donald on a hostility scale.

People in the first group who had searched for the names of hostile people rated Donald as less hostile—after all, anyone would be rated as less hostile than someone like Adolph Hitler or Charlie Manson. People in the second group who had searched for names of gentle people saw Donald as more hostile—after all, anyone would be rated as more hostile than Peter Pan or Santa Claus.

The two groups then participated in a bargaining game with someone who they were led to believe was Donald. In the game, they had the option of being cooperative or competitive. Those who had seen Donald as more hostile were more likely to choose competition, while those who saw Donald as less hostile were more likely to choose cooperation.

The context of my perception even influences me on simple things, like looking at a picture. I can't resist showing you the following example of just how true this statement is. Look at the illustration of the clown below.

Can you see the clown? See anything else? If you can only see the clown, look at the image below and see what you may have missed.

Can you now see the circus scene? Can you see those tightrope walkers, the seal, and the man on the unicycle? And what about the horses?

This is a terrific example of how "orientation" relates to the context. How I position myself—which goes back to my discussion on assumptions and beliefs—sets a context that influences what I see.

Here's a final example. I've had so much fun with this over the years. What do you see in this next illustration?

Can you see the image of a female? What would you say is the generic age of the female in this illustration? Did you see a young woman or an old woman? Or did your perception flip back and forth, so you saw both? I've flashed this picture to audiences in different contexts. In one group, I was talking a lot about youth, about the challenge for young people today. Most of that group saw a picture of a young woman.

In another session, I was talking about Halloween and witches and goblins. Wouldn't you know it? That group saw an old woman. Context sure is a powerful influence on perception!

By the way, perception does not only refer to sight. Hearing is also a type of perception. A good example of internal influences on hearing might be a male doctor on call sitting at home with his wife. He may hear the sound of a phone ringing before the crying of his baby, but his wife might do just the opposite.

The fact is, my perception of anything is influenced by space and time, as well as the limitations of my objective sensors. I can only see so far, I can only smell so much in the moment. I can only sense so many vibrations of light and sound. However I am also limited by what *I think* about what I see, taste, hear, smell, and touch.

I often hear the adage, "perception is everything." This phrase is uttered with such authority as though to suggest there is no other way to understand it. I do not think it is just that simple. Although I am always relying on my interpretation of the vibrations I receive through my objective sensors, I contend it is extremely important for me to understand I can not count only on what my senses bring to me. All of this causes me to wonder if there is a subtle but important distinction between reality and actuality.

The definition of actuality is something that is real, as opposed to what is expected, intended, or feared.

One definition of reality states: the totality of real things in the world, independent of people's knowledge or perception of them.

On the surface they both come down to "what is real." However, if I accept the contentions that a) my objective senses are limited and b) I am limited by what I think, then it seems to me that my interpretation of what is real can at times be tainted.

Therefore the more I can understand my beliefs, my experiences, and how my cultural points of view influence my perceptions, the better my chances are of being in touch with a more complete view of my actuality which may be somewhat different than what I am realizing. This is a distinction worthy of pondering.

Other Influences on My Perception

My beliefs are not the only thing affecting how I perceive. My values, needs, emotions, interests, attitudes, and expectations all influence my perception.

For example, in one study, researchers asked children to judge the size of coins. Children from poor families saw the coins larger than did children from affluent families.

In a very interesting study, a researcher sent two teams of boys at a summer camp on a jelly bean hunt. When they came back into the dining room, he led them in a guessing game. He dumped each boy's bag of jelly beans on an overhead projector, flashed the light on and off, and asked all of them to guess how many jelly beans were in the bag. Unknown to them, he used his own bag each time, with a constant number of jelly beans, instead of a boy's bag. The findings were dramatic. The more status (popularity, respect, etc.) a boy had among members of his team, the higher the number of jelly beans was perceived. And, overall, each team saw their members as collecting more jelly beans than the members of the other team!

Perceptions are also influenced by prejudices. Particular groupings of people—New Yorkers, street people, people from the Middle East, teenagers, Blacks, Hispanics, Chinese, football players, and so on—immediately bring clusters of characteristics about them to people's minds. The associations I have learned to make when encountering various groups of people have become so automatic I often don't realize just how much they are influencing my here-and-now perceptions.

Examples of how my own internal state influences what I perceive are all around me. You've heard the expression, "Love is blind." Being in love myself, there is no doubt my partner is more beautiful than anyone else. Or how about the time I see someone who reminds me of someone else I knew in the past. If the person I knew was a wonderful person, I tend to see the new person favorably. If the person I knew was not a wonderful person, I tend to see the new person less favorably.

Perception and My Memory: Visualization

How and what I perceive is important to my central tool of memory. To remember something I first have to pay attention to it, in other words, perceive it. Many things influence how I perceive something.

I'm going to concentrate here on *visual perception*. I will present information about hearing in the next chapter on listening.

I start by being aware of how my perceptions are influenced. When my awareness leads me to stop and think about what I am seeing, I can improve the accuracy of my perceptions.

When I ask my friends to join me in perceiving a variety of people and things and compare what I perceive to what they perceive, I find myself uncovering some of the beliefs and assumptions that influence my perceptions.

I train myself to visualize. This was a bit more difficult for me because I do not favor visual memory (as described in chapter 5 where I talked about NLP). My predominant modality is auditory. However, visualization is a very helpful technique for remembering and is involved in several of the memory exercises that I have presented in this book.

Also, in chapter 5 I described an exercise I use to enhance my level of concentration. The same concept can be used to practice visualization.

As with the concentration exercise I hold in my hands a small object I have around my house. It may be a flashlight, a lamp, or perhaps a box of Kleenex. I focus on the object for several seconds. I note its size, its shape, its colors, and its texture.

I put the object out of sight. I sit back and close my eyes and visualize the object for several seconds, trying to recreate every detail I can in my mind's eye.

I then open my eyes and write down as detailed a description as I can of the object—I even create a drawing of it sometimes to help me reconstruct it more vividly.

I check my notes against the actual object. Often, the first time I do this, I miss details. So I do it again.

I repeat the process until I am satisfied with the clarity of my visualization.

I go through the same steps with other objects throughout the course of my day. When I am a passenger in a moving car (not, of course, if I'm the driver), I visualize other vehicles or passing scenery in the same way. At work, I visualize the people around me.

In other words, I practice these steps alternately visualizing and checking the accuracy of my visualizations in many situations at different times of the day.

One thing that helps me visualize is learning how to relax myself into a quiet state of meditation. Several years ago, I learned to do this by leaning back, closing my eyes, taking several slow, deep breaths, and gradually visualizing the colors of the rainbow. Some people will recall striking sunsets or other beautiful sights they have experienced.

One more thing I want to note about perception. I believe many people don't go through their days open to experimenting with their lives doing new things and looking at new ideas, fueled by an eagerness to learn. That "perception"—that eagerness to learn and see my life as an adventure—makes me much more open to being present and therefore conscious about what is going on around me.

If I can enhance my ability to perceive more accurately, well then, surely I am going to be more open to other possibilities. I will have taken the first step to doing things that now seem impossible, like reading another person's mind.

CHAPTER EIGHT

Listening: I Hear What I Want to Hear

> One of the best ways to persuade others is with your ears by listening to them.
> —*Dean Rusk (1909-1994)*
> *U.S. Secretary of State (1961-69)*

Still another very important source of sensory input to me is how I listen to people. I can choose to *hear* what someone says, or I can choose to truly *listen* to what someone says. I have found there is a big difference between the two.

Let me begin by offering you a quick quiz. Write down your answer beside each method of communicating.

Writing			
Reading			
Speaking			
Listening			

Here is the first question. What percent of time do you think people generally spend in each of these four ways of communicating? And keep in mind your answer should add up to 100 percent. Write your answer in the first column.

The second question is: How many years of formal training do you believe most people receive in each of these four ways of communicating? Write your answers next to the percentages in the second column.

Here is question number three. In the third column write down what you think is the average listening efficiency of most people—I will make this a multiple-choice question. Is it 15 percent, 25 percent, 60 percent, or 75 percent?

Based on my research for this topic the percentages of time most people spend engaged in each activity, and the years of training received for each of the four ways of communicating are:

Writing	9%	12 Years	
Reading	16%	6-8 Years	
Speaking	35%	1-2 Years	
Listening	40%	0 Years	Efficiency 25%

And here is the real kicker: the average listening efficiency of most people is *only 25 percent!*

Isn't that amazing? I spend such a large amount of my waking time listening, yet I was taught to read, write, and speak, but rarely to listen. In fact, it's said children's listening skills actually decline as they grow older.

Good listening really does take time, but I just never seem to have enough time to hear the whole story. Perhaps it's because I live in such a fast-paced world. It seems as though I'm always in a hurry. I often find myself self-talking and saying, "Get on with it. Please get to the point! I don't need to hear every detail." Of course the truth be known, I often inaccurately think I know the person's point. To make it worse, while I'm screaming in my mind, "Please get to the point," I'm missing the very point the person I'm pretending to listen to is making.

Also, most people think listening is boring. It's more fun to talk. In fact, for many people, the opposite of talking is not listening—it's waiting to talk. I think you will agree many times we just don't listen very well. It's the main reason many people have trouble remembering names.

Effective listening is a learned and trained skill. It is a discipline. I must always be willing and mentally focused to listen, accept, interact with, and absorb the information being imparted to me.

Trying to remember information when I listen to someone is directly influenced by the effectiveness of my skill at listening. The basic problem is it's a skill I take for granted. I don't even think about it. As an adult, I don't usually question my ability to listen. After all, haven't I been listening all of my life? I have two ears, and they receive sounds.

The fact is, even before I could talk, I was listening. Without even paying attention, I listen. Every moment of every day, I listen without giving it a thought. But here's the point: listening without thinking is ineffective listening. And ineffective listening gets in the way of remembering things.

Effective listening is careful, concentrated, and focused listening. It is not automatic. It is a skill that is developed and sharpened. It takes practice—a great deal of practice.

The more effectively I listen, the more effectively I will remember, whether it is people's names, information about them, information about my business, etc. The more I understand what someone is saying—what he or she is implying, what he or she is feeling, what he or she wants and hopes and wishes for—the more effectively I will remember what I want to remember from the interaction. Understanding truly requires skilled listening

Active Listening and the *Effective Listening Pyramid*

Experts refer to skilled listening as "active" listening. Active listening is listening *with* instead of listening *to* another person. This means I actively participate with the person to whom I am listening.

Relaxed and alert, I establish good eye contact, I concentrate on listening, and I pay attention to voice tones and inflections, facial expressions, body movements, and especially, eye movements. I use every sense at my disposal to perceive and understand what the other person is saying.

The most effective listening is done while I am in what psychologists call the "Adult Ego State." This is a problem-solving state of mind, when I am being strictly logical, unfettered by my emotional and judgmental filters.

While in this state, I am also more capable of seeing around the other person's filters. I see him/her with more clarity. I am receptive. I am analytical. I am more likely to understand the link between what he/she is feeling and the words he/she is saying.

Given that effective listening is a learned skill, what steps can you and I take to learn it? How do we go about developing such a skill?

Well, below is what I think of as the Effective Listening Pyramid.

The Effective Listening Pyramid consists of six steps:

6- Listen With Empathy
5- Listen Analytically
4- Listen Objectively
3- Observe Nonverbal Behavior
2- Pay Attention
1- Stop Talking

If I practice these six steps, working my way up the pyramid, I will soon improve my level of listening skills. Now, I want to take a few moments to understand the impact of these six steps to effective listening.

The First Step in Effective Listening:

I Am Committed to Stop Talking

The hardest thing for me to learn is to stop talking, and was I born to talk! But how can I possibly listen to someone when I am so busy talking? The fact of the matter is I almost never learn anything while I am talking.

I was reinforced to talk from the beginning—way back in the crib. When I was just a baby lying alone in my crib with nobody around, I was not getting any attention. But the minute I started crying, people came running—I got attention! Someone picked me up and comforted me and attended to my needs. I "spoke" and got rewarded.

When I spoke my very first words, that special moment for parents, I know I got major attention. Then, as I formed sentences and came up with cute remarks, even more attention—smiles and "Oh, isn't that sweet." In grammar school, when my teacher called on me to recite and complimented me for my performance, I felt rewarded. Even when I didn't say it right, the relief I felt when it was over was rewarding.

Over and over again, as I grew into adulthood, I was reinforced when I spoke, by the facial expressions of others and by their approving nods and comments.

As an adult, I often talk too much because I am anxious to convince someone of something. Or I want to make a sale. Or I want to show someone how right I am about something, and so on. In other words, I am busy pushing my own agenda. This is something I learned from my earliest years. To overcome this tendency, I dedicate myself to receiving information instead of sending it—I focus on listening to other people's communication. I attempt to understand their agenda.

I also sometimes talk too much because I am uncomfortable with someone else's silence or nonresponsiveness when I am talking to them. Over the years, I've learned to deal with that feeling of discomfort by "filling in the empty space," by talking.

To break that habit, I take a deep breath and realize many people I listen to stop and think before speaking. I must give them the opportunity to do so.

With both of these forces driving me to talk, it's no wonder I find it hard to stop and just listen.

The Second Step in Effective Listening:

I Am Committed to Pay Attention

This means many things. I must concentrate on what the other person is saying. I should not fidget. People passing by should not distract me. I should not let extraneous noises like telephones, people talking, and heavy trucks rumbling nearby pull my attention away from the person to whom I am listening.

In addition, when I have a choice, I choose my time of day. I have more energy at certain times of the day than I do at other times of the day.

Energy is very important, because when I feel fatigued, it interferes with my ability to concentrate. When I am very tired, I find it harder to pay attention. I find it all too easy to just drift, thinking about other matters; or I just begin to daydream.

Energy levels aren't just determined by the time of the day. Dealing with some acute personal problem, for example, drains energy. This weakens my focus on paying attention to the person to whom I am listening. I know I do my best listening when I am not preoccupied with personal dilemmas.

There's still another factor that interferes with my paying attention. I have a habit of finishing people's sentences for them. Can you relate? Well, it's not that I'm a rude person. It's more a matter of time and capacity.

Consider that the number of words I can think per minute is well over twice the number I can speak per minute. This means my mind needs less than half the time to listen to what the other person is saying. During the rest of the time, my thoughts wander. I daydream. I think about something I did this morning or what I need to do later. I think about some personal problem. Compared to the speed of my thinking, the other person is speaking in slow motion.

To overcome this factor, I need to mentally review what I am hearing, organize it, and attach it to other things I know.

Given these forces working against paying attention, it's no wonder I have difficulty keeping my focus on what I am hearing.

The Third Step in Effective Listening:

I Am Committed to Observe Nonverbal Messages

An effective listener "listens" to more than just words. Research has shown only a third of my communication comes from words—the rest comes from nonverbal messages—a fleeting expression, a tightening of muscles, a lifting of eyebrows, a change in body posture. As I described when discussing NLP, I especially observe eye movements. I listen to the tone, inflections, pitch, and timbre of the voice of the person talking to me. All of these actions tell me something about the internal state of mind of the person to whom I am listening.

It is much easier for me to choose what words I use when talking than it is for me to control my physical reactions. Often what I say is contradicted by how I act. Even the size of the pupils of my eyes is affected by my feelings. For example, when I am surprised or afraid, my pupils dilate; when I am calculating or concentrating, they contract.

I practice observing nonverbal cues, and I find myself taking in more information—more accurate information—hence, listening and remembering more effectively.

The Fourth Step in Effective Listening:

I Am Committed to Listen Objectively

Communication between me and another person passes through a number of "filters," such as my beliefs, the critical  judgments I make, and the way I feel about the person speaking or what he or she is saying. At times those filters are so strong I hear something other than what is being said, or I even fail to hear anything at all. I filter what I hear through my beliefs, my knowledge about what I am hearing, and the meanings I give to words, meanings I learned through experience. My experience is different from the experience of others. The meaning I give to a word or phrase may be very different from the meaning someone else gives to that word or phrase. As one expert on listening mused, "meanings are not in words, meanings are in people."

In fact, just last week I had an experience with my two daughters, which if left untended, might have developed into a very unhappy situation. It all had to do with the interpretation of a single phrase.

I made a statement suggesting that I understood my two-year-old grandson, Zane Anton, was too young to not throw a temper tantrum. "In fact," I continued, "even my five-year-old granddaughter, Jessica, still throws a tantrum when she does not get her way. But Zane will pass this stage and all will be well."

It turned out one of my daughters heard my statement—minus the word "even" and had an entirely different interpretation of my comment.

Fortunately, we talked it through, my meaning became clear, and we avoided some hurt feelings.

To minimize the influence of these filters when I listen, I train myself to listen objectively. This means, as I noted earlier, I listen from my adult ego state, so I can process what I hear without weighing it down with evaluative judgments.

Well-known psychologist Carl Rogers asserted that our tendency to evaluate is the biggest barrier to effective communication. It is impossible to hear objectively when I am making critical judgments about the speaker.

I listen objectively by suspending my judgments when I listen. I consciously put my beliefs aside. I listen logically, not by evaluating what the speaker is saying.

The Fifth Step in Effective Listening:

I Am Committed to Listen Analytically

Sometimes people appear to be unorganized or fuzzy minded when they describe something to me. They tend to ramble or talk in circles, and I have a hard time following them.

This happens with some people who are compulsive—who want to make sure every relevant point is covered. It also happens to some people who are nervous because they really don't have a handle on what they want to say—they don't want to be perceived as stupid or uninformed, so they ramble around in their talking. In either case, the person has something to say. So I must resist the temptation to consider what they are saying as unimportant, drifting off into my own mental self-talk—I would not then be effectively listening and would entirely miss whatever is being said.

I can listen more effectively by listening analytically—by identifying themes and grouping what is being said around a few key ideas.

I organize what I hear as I go along. I mentally review. I listen for details. I fill in with supporting facts. The burden is on me, as the listener, to make sense out of what the other person is saying.

The Sixth Step in Effective Listening:

I Am Committed to Listen with Empathy

The word "empathy" comes from a German word *einfühlung* which means "feeling into." An example of my listening with empathy is when I find myself choking up as I watch someone who is crying over the loss of a loved one.

Another example is when I lean forward in my seat at the movies, all tensed up as I watch a hero struggling through a tough situation.

The empathic listener tries to feel the world as the speaker feels it. In other words, the empathic listener feels the world from the speaker's point of view. This does not mean I lose my own objectivity or personal point of view. It means I train myself to put myself into the speaker's shoes—to vicariously experience the speaker's internal feelings.

Listening with empathy has a special side effect. The more I am able to listen with empathy, the more I put a person at ease. The more I put people at ease, the easier it is for them to speak, the more they will open up to me, the more I will learn about them, and thus, the more effectively I will listen.

Practice Effective Listening

Building effective listening skills takes practice. Simply listening to someone is not enough. Truly effective listening requires me to train myself in the six steps described above. Practice, practice, and practice some more.

Every time I listen to someone, I picture in my mind the Effective Listening Pyramid.

I've created a useful exercise to help you practice.

You'll need someone to be your partner, a copy of the Effective Listening Pyramid, a copy of the four questions below for each of you, a tape recorder, and a TV.

Seat yourselves comfortably in front of the TV.

Go over the four questions together, noting how they fit with the steps on the Effective Listening Pyramid.

Then tune into one of the many talk shows on TV. Pick a starting point—preferably when someone has been asked a question—turn on your tape recorder, and start listening, keeping the steps of the Effective Listening Pyramid in mind.

As you listen, remember first and foremost to *stop talking and pay attention!*

> 1. Describe as many nonverbal behaviors as you can, remember and discuss what meaning they gave to what the person was saying.
>
> 2. Note the judgements you made as you listened and what you thought about them at the time.
>
> 3. What was the central theme or main point the speaker was making?
>
> 4. Describe how you would feel being that person.

After listening for three minutes or so, mute the TV, and stop the tape recorder. Compare what you heard to what your partner heard by asking each other the four questions.

If you disagree with each other about what you heard, play the tape recorder to check it out.

Repeat this exercise several times.

Keep at it to sharpen your ability to pick up nonverbal cues, to make yourself aware of judgments you make and how they might interfere with your listening effectiveness, to organize what you are hearing so you can clearly identify what is being said, and to fine-tune your ability to listen with empathy.

A Final Look at the Effective Listening Pyramid

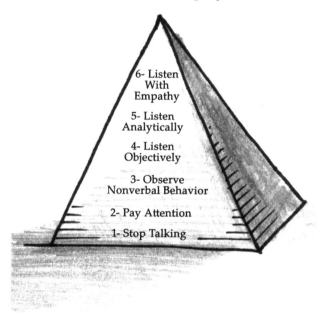

I know from my personal experience that building my effective listening skill continues to take a lot of practice.

CHAPTER NINE

Intuition: My Other Sense

> I never came upon any of my discoveries through the process of rational thinking.
> —*Albert Einstein (1879-1955)*
> *Mathematician and physicist*

A brief recap is in order. To this point I have expressed my thoughts about perception, demonstrated how my perception is influenced by my beliefs and assumptions, described the Effective Listening Pyramid along with my views about the relationship of listening and memory.

However, there is still one additional important sense I wish to discuss. Some people refer to it as our "sixth sense." Others refer to this sense as intuition. And many discount the notion of its existence at all.

"What?" I can almost see you looking at me with a skeptical smile. "Are you talking about clairvoyance? About mental telepathy? About psychics?"

No, not at all.

Actually I'm referring to a source of a sensory process as real and as legitimate as perception and listening. A sense many people have not trained themselves to use. Unfortunately, people tend to discount the very notion of intuition, mainly because it is usually looked upon as unscientific and speculative.

In reality, the concept of intuition is much older than our current views of psychics. Intuition is as old as the Pythagorean theorem. The Greek philosopher Pythagoras and his followers made much use of it to establish their rules of mathematics. Intuition also was important to religious thinkers down through the ages, as a way of knowing God.

Over the centuries, ethical philosophers talked about intuition as a way of "knowing moral values." Spinoza regarded intuition as the "highest form of knowledge" that permits our mind "to be a part of the Infinite Being." Kant saw intuition as "the portion of perception that is supplied by the mind itself" to help us understand the sensations we experience from external objects. Bergson regarded intuition as "the purest form of instinct."

Today, science rules. We have improved our material lives and have expanded our understanding of our world—our universe—through the application of scientific methods. Our belief systems today are embedded in scientific thinking. Intuition is consigned to the worlds of religion, philosophy, and mysticism.

Yet every one of us has had experiences in our lives we call intuitive. I've often said to myself when disappointed in something someone does, "I had a gut feeling not to trust that guy!"

Or how about the time I answered a telephone, and I knew who was calling—without caller ID—before the person ever spoke?

Then there's the time I said to myself, "I just knew that was going to happen!"

My conjecture is any one of you reading this book could come up with many examples of intuitive sensing.

Another problem is these experiences seem to be random and unanticipated. Many people write them off to chance. Some, in fact, may be due to chance. But are all of them due to chance? I don't think so.

Maybe what happens in those "intuitive" instances is I utilize a sense I haven't formally trained myself to use. Perhaps I should look at intuition as a personal skill I can develop if I just choose to. It would be worthwhile if I could make it a conscious part of my daily living!

I believe I can. Furthermore, I am certain my intuition is one of the most useful of my senses. It is the key to being able to read my own mind and perhaps the minds of others.

Intuition sits at the top of all of the mind skills I've been talking about in the previous chapters. It is a special sensory skill that helps me give meaning to all of the information I absorb every day through all of my other senses. At any given moment, I see, hear, feel, touch, taste, and smell more than I realize. Could it be that intuition quickly helps me grasp it all?

But What Do I Really Propose by "Intuition"?

Intuition has been defined or described dozens of ways by philosophers and psychologists. Allow me to quote a few.

The second college edition of Webster's New World Dictionary dictionary defines "intuition" as: (l) the immediate knowing or learning of something without the conscious use of reasoning. (2) In its cognitive function it is a psychic organ or means to apprehend reality. It is a synthetic function in the sense that it apprehends the totality of a given situation or psychological reality. It does not work from the part to the whole—as the analytical mind does—but apprehends a totality directly in its living existence (Assagioli *http://pespmc1.vub.ac.be/ASC/INTUITION.html*). (3) It is by logic that we prove, but by intuition that we discover (Poincare, *cy* sq. *Web Dictionary of Cybernetics and Systems*).

I believe we all have the capability of embracing and enhancing our intuitive ability. I grew up with the false notion that only women had intuition. I suppose it was because of often hearing the phrases "woman's intuition" and "a mother's instinct" as if men did not have it. Of course we do—we just call it by a different name. Men call it "a hunch" or "a gut feeling."

For me, intuition is what I know because of who I am and who I will become. Intuition is what I know for sure but not for certain.

Intuition is a way of knowing, an unconscious assembling of sensory perceptions into meaningful patterns and predictions, and arriving at conclusions without having "analyzed" the facts—a true "gut feeling."

So what really happens when I get that "gut feeling" about something or someone? What causes me to know almost instantly as in a flash, a solution to some question or problem?

My personal interpretation of how my intuition process works is that my mind is rapidly connecting sensations and information into new patterns of meaning. I reach conclusions so rapidly I don't even know how I do it. An unconscious part of my brain is at work. Perhaps one of the keys to "tuning up" my intuitive abilities is to learn how to bring this process into my consciousness.

I intend to fully explain my thinking and methods for consciously influencing the use of my intuition, but first I want to share a couple of stories that I think are very good examples of the power and effect of acting on what may at the time merely seem like flashes of intuition.

A Real-Life Example of Conscious Intuition

I can't think of a more dramatic example of using both my logical analytical thinking along with my intuitive skills than how my wife, Lois, and I first met and began our near-thirty-year relationship together.

On the next few pages Lois and I are going to relate the story of how we first met. We will each recount our story from our own perspective. I think this will provide a more vivid accounting of how—although we come from totally different backgrounds, and we think so differently—we were brought together by individual circumstances (perhaps intuitive in nature) so we could provide balance to each other's lives. While I am more earthly and usually function in a more logical and cautious frame of mind, Lois is more intuitive and easily calls upon her spiritual and gentler nature. I am working at developing and utilizing these important qualities.

Lois's Perspective

In the fall of 1975 a male friend and I were on a vacation trip that ended rather abruptly. During this period in my life my belief system included the thought that nothing was coincidental, but instead I believed all things happen for a purpose. So, as I was traveling home, I decided to pay attention to my thinking and my feelings so I could learn what I felt drawn to do for the remainder of my vacation time.

I may not have consciously known it at the time, but what was happening was I was suspending judgment about the early ending of my trip, and I began to mentally ask questions of myself. The result of this mental exercise was that I met the man who would become my husband, Anton Zellmann. The following story describes my perspective of how our meeting took place.

When I returned home from my trip, it occurred to me to phone a good friend of mine to whom I had not spoken for a few months. While we were talking, I asked her to meet with me and to go shopping at a local shopping center. This may seem like a typical activity for many women, but it was not typical of me. Nor was it typical of me to call this particular friend, and ask her to go shopping with me. Even though this was totally impulsive of me, it felt like the perfect thing to do so I went with it. We agreed to meet, set the time, and I was off to Southwick Shopping Center in Toledo, Ohio.

When I arrived, I looked at the large sign used to announce any special activity that might be taking place in the center. The message read "Entertainment in ESP" featuring Anton Zellman. I became very excited. Mostly because at the time, I worked for a personal effectiveness training company that taught people how to understand that they were responsible for their thoughts and actions, as well as how to use their psychic and intuitive abilities. As I read the sign I knew this was exactly why I was drawn to this particular place. It was to meet this man who was performing ESP demonstrations.

I met up with my friend, Marilyn, and told her I would like to see this guy who was going to perform at the fountain area in the shopping center. We joined the crowd waiting to see the show. And then there he was. He began to talk with a calming and mesmerizing voice. The show was fun to watch, and the man was absolutely amazing. He was actually demonstrating some of the concepts we were teaching at our training center. Both Marilyn and I were having a really good time. When Zellman asked for a group of volunteers, I agreed eagerly. I don't remember exactly what I did during his demonstration, but I do recall I was in awe that he was able to accomplish what he said he would do.

When the show was over, my friend and I went into Friendly's restaurant to have lunch. As we sat there, we noticed Zellman standing at the cash register with his back to us. We decided to test his mind-reading abilities by mentally sending him suggestions to come over to our table.

Imagine our surprise when he turned around and walked directly over to our table and said, "Excuse me, you ladies called me over?" We started to laugh with amazement and delight.

We talked for a few minutes. I told him how much we enjoyed his show and that we worked for a company that helped people to tap into their own psychic abilities. He didn't seem very interested, but we traded business cards, and he left the restaurant.

I couldn't get this experience off my mind. It had such a huge impact on me. The next day I typed out a letter to Anton Zellman stating I thought we could do some great things together. I was thinking in terms of doing personal growth training. I later learned he thought I was coming on to him. As it turned out, I suppose it was both though I was not conscious of it at the time. Actually it was probably more prophetic than a come-on.

About a week later I was talking with another friend and telling her how much I wanted to have a relationship with a guy, but I was having trouble finding any men who seemed interested in me. It was during that conversation when Anton called and asked me to go out to dinner with him.

As I look back at this situation, the processes Anton is talking about in his chapter on intuition abound. When my trip plans changed, I immediately observed my thoughts. What Anton refers to as "being present." I knew something was up since, as I mentioned, I do not believe in coincidence. My mind-set was such that I was open to new thoughts and new solutions. I believe everything has a purpose and consequence.

As I began to observe my thoughts I also asked good questions of myself. "What did I feel like doing?" "Why was I home early from my planned vacation?" When the idea of calling Marilyn came up, I could feel in my body it was a right choice. I trusted my intuition, and I acted on it.

When I chose to go to the exact place at which Anton was appearing, arrived at the exact time he was about to perform his ESP show, and then we saw him at the restaurant, I knew it had meaning. Even though my interpretation was skewed. I really did not know we would have a personal relationship. We seemed so different from each other, and we are, but what did I know?

After I acted on my intuition, went to the shopping center, and met Anton, I then took an action by sending him a follow-up letter. I felt it was important for us to get together and talk. I did not know exactly why or how it would work out, but I knew I wanted to follow it through. Also, the timing of Anton's call to ask me out just as I was talking about dating pretty much sealed it. I knew I was supposed to go out with this guy.

But as mature, smart, and perceptive as I thought I was at twenty-three years of age, I still did not get it. You see, I stood Anton up on that first date. If it were not for Anton's patience, wisdom (he was ten years older), kindness, and his mental capacity to see beyond the immediate issue of being stood up, we may not have had the opportunity to spend the past wonderful twenty-nine years together! Anton truly is psychic and has the capacity to read minds . . . at the very least I know he can read me like a book.

Anton's Perspective

My first marriage of fourteen years was, to say the least, tumultuous. Our separation and later our divorce began on September 7, 1975. And you can be certain the last thing on my mind was to look for or begin another relationship. All I wanted to do was take some time to calm down, to reflect, and to heal.

I realized most of my income from my sales job with the Bulova Watch Company would and should go to the continuing support of my soon-to-be former wife and our two daughters. So I needed to supplement my income.

That same year I began to think seriously about developing a sideline business performing as a "mentalist," demonstrating what appear to be extraordinary feats of *mental* or *psychic* skills.

I launched a campaign to market myself in the Toledo, Ohio, area as a man who could perform these mental miracles. I billed myself as the "Master of Mental Fun" and as a "Magician of the Mind." I performed without pay at local events, and in a short amount of time I managed to convince local businesses to pay for my entertainment services.

One day I was driving by a shopping center and noticed a billboard announcing a puppet show and a magician were performing inside the center. I decided to check it out.

As I watched the show, a light bulb (intuition?) went off in my mind. Why not sell the shopping center management on having me perform at some future event? I thought it over and came up with an idea for a special event. I located the shopping center's manager and presented my idea to conduct a storewide promotion, which I named ESP Weekend at Southwick Center. ESP meant an "**E**xciting **S**ales **P**romotion with Extra-**S**pecial **P**rices and Extra-**S**ensational **P**rizes." The manager liked the idea and hired me to perform my show, "Entertainment in ESP" three times a day for three days the weekend of September 20, 1975 (less than two weeks after my separation).

Since I was still rather new at performing as a "mentalist" and a shopping center was a new venue for me, I spent a lot of my time onstage focused on what I was doing, where I was

standing, what I would say next, and so on. As a result, I really didn't pay much attention to the audience or to the volunteers who came onstage to assist me in my mental demonstrations. Today, I am more confident about my speaking and mentalist skills so I experience the pleasure and joy of observing my audience observe me.

On the last day of my engagement, having seven shows under my belt, I was feeling very relaxed and on top of my game. Just before delivering my second presentation on the last day of the promotion, I walked into a restaurant in the shopping center for a takeout cup of coffee. As I paid for my coffee and turned to leave, I noticed two women sitting in a nearby booth. I believe their eyes were closed, as though they were concentrating.

Without any notion of what I might say to them, I felt compelled to approach them. So I walked over to their table. As I approached, they opened their eyes. "You ladies wanted to speak with me?" I asked with a smile.

Their mouths fell open. They began to smile, and then they laughed loudly. As it turned out, they both worked for a company that taught mind concepts, how to take responsibility for one's thinking, and how to tap into unused mental (psychic) potential.

The ladies had just seen my ESP show. In fact, I later learned one of them gave me a pen to use during my mind-reading demonstration. (I promise you I did not consciously realize this when I first approached them.)

They told me they recognized me when I came in for coffee and decided they would test me to see if I was really a mind reader, if I could really intuitively know they wanted to talk with me. So they closed their eyes and concentrated on calling me over.

Well, one of them was Lois, my dear friend and wife for the past twenty-nine years. The rest is history.

Intuition Works

My intuition was surely working for me that afternoon. Of course, I realize I might have unconsciously recognized them or I might have "read" some kind of body language. Perhaps I just saw two pretty women and came up with the best line of my life—"You ladies wanted to speak with me?" Whatever the trigger, something told me to walk over to them. I paid attention to and acted on my thoughts. The benefit of that action has brought years of happiness and joy into my life and the lives of my children and our grandchildren.

Early on in our relationship, Lois and I agreed that if one of us had a "hit" (meaning we experienced an intuitive moment), then we would discuss it and support each other rather than denigrate the intuitive experience. We would never discount the other's experience with typical comments such as "Oh, that was just a coincidence," or "What a flake you are, that stuff doesn't work, don't be so naive." I believe this mutual support helps us to enjoy a great many more accurate "hits" together.

I believe it is on target to conclude that there were several similar key components in both of our stories about how we met, to suggest more was at work than both of us merely making isolated choices. Based on many conversations with Lois about our meeting I am certain we both used, in our individual ways, our intuitive abilities. I will explain this further when I present my two-phase system for "tuning up" and "tapping into" what I think of as my conscious use of intuition. First, I want to share one more story I believe supports my theory about conscious use of intuition.

Could It Be Simply Another Habit?

A friend of mine, Arnie Dahlke, recently told me about a habit of his that makes for another really good example of conscious intuition in action. He told me he frequently wakes up in the morning, and while lying relaxed in bed, the complete solution to a problem he had been wrestling with for days pops into his mind. He believes that's his intuition at work.

Arnie also told me about a dramatic daytime experience he recalls. He had been working for weeks on the research design for his doctoral dissertation in social psychology. He had become absolutely stuck in his attempts to solve a particular design problem. He knew if he didn't solve his problem, he would be unable to conduct his research.

He became more anxious as the days went by.

Finally, one weekend, Arnie decided he had had enough. It was time to kick back and relax a bit. Being a fan of science fiction novels, he picked up a novel he had been reading and became totally immersed in it.

He had been reading for over an hour when something dramatic occurred. Arnie had a flash of insight. What is commonly referred to as an "aha" experience.

He explained he was reading a sentence describing a mental battle between the hero and the villain when, suddenly, the entire solution to his research problem popped full blown into his mind! He put his novel down, picked up a pad of paper, and sketched it out.

The solution worked. He went on to conduct his research and finish his dissertation.

Notice something very important in this example of paying attention to intuition. In this situation, Arnie was in a relaxed mental state of mind. He was totally relaxed and absorbed in his book when he had his aha experience. The first three steps I use to cultivate my intuition—suspending my assumptions and judgments, totally relaxing myself physically, and clearing my mind of self-talk—are essential to opening me up to intuitive experiences.

Arnie, who conducts training seminars and workshops, tells me that now when he is working on a new topic, he will take himself out to a nice, long lunch, accompanied by a novel and a notepad. Sometimes, he'll start with a glass of wine, reading his novel as he begins to eat. Invariably, at some point during the lunch, he finds ideas popping into his head. He grabs his notebook or tape recorder and starts working. He has designed many sessions in that manner! In fact, it has become his habit to do so.

Once I learned to cultivate my intuition and practice using it over and over again, I found intuiting had become just another one of my habits as well. Remarkably, I have observed myself having what seems like many more intuitive experiences without consciously thinking about doing so.

Creating a New Mind-Set

So how do I cultivate my intuition, my subliminal mind-reading skill? I've often stated during my presentations, "I believe any one who chooses to can develop their skill of intuition." In order to demonstrate my belief I am going to present a two-phase process designed by my wife, Lois, and me, which we use to prepare for and cultivate our intuitive ability. Each phase has a series of components I find helpful in "tuning up" and "tapping into" my intuitive ability.

As with many of the exercises in this book, it takes so much longer to describe than to do. Once understood and practiced, the following process takes less than a minute or two to accomplish.

Overview—Honing My Intuitive Process

I regard the components of Phase One as a means of "tuning up and training" my intuitive processing. After all, if I have not been intentionally using this untapped mental resource—if it has been dormant for most, if not all of my life—then surely I must do something to awaken it, and then exercise this "sensory muscle" that has been in a state of atrophy for many years from lack of use.

To accomplish this, I initiate Phase One, consisting of the following three actions, in preparation for Phase Two.

1. I relax my mind and my body.
2. I suspend my assumptions and judgments—the "rules" that keep me from "thinking outside the box."
3. I become consciously present and I actively initiate my mind to be present, observing and opening myself to intuitive experiences.

Now I am ready to begin Phase Two, which is designed to cultivate and exercise my innate power of intuition.

- I observe and discern my self-talk.
- I mentally ask questions.
- I observe and discern my answers.
- I check any noticeable results.
- I practice, practice, and practice some more.

A Closer Look

The image of the crystal ball to the right helps to illustrate the inherent qualities in developing and activating a mind-set that supports the maturity of a more conscious use of my intuition. It depicts a mixture of all of the components utilized in this two-phase process.

It is important to stress that Phase Two is not a structure composed of a number of orderly steps but instead is made up of a variety of free-flowing components.

This is not always a linear process, but instead, it is an ever-evolving mind-set with components that are fluid and in motion rather than exact and consistent in its order of occurrence. At any moment in time I may enter into the process through the same or a different component.

These components flow freely in a random mixture and allow for intuitive insight to activate during any part of the process. Is this not true intuition? The unexpected, or perhaps it is truly the expected, arrival of a new idea, a new solution, or a new insight, without any constriction from logic or reasoning.

Accompany me now as I guide you through this process. And again, please keep in mind, even though my explanation of each phase and its components may take you several minutes to read and to comprehend, after some limited practice the entire process will take but moments to accomplish.

Phase One: Prepare Physically and Mentally

I Relax My Body and Mind

This is not a long, drawn-out process. It is simply a matter of calming my mind and body through proper breathing.

I notice my breathing. I breathe in and out, slowly and steadily. I breathe in the same manner as a sleeping baby. The baby's abdomen expands as it inhales and the abdomen contracts as it exhales. This is a correct breathing habit. Breathing from the diaphragm rather than the chest.

Breathing from the diaphragm produces the equivalent of a relaxation response. My heart rate and blood pressure will drop, and I become composed and confident. I am in total control.

I feel the air coming into and flooding my lungs as I breathe inward. I hold my breath for a couple of seconds. I feel the oxygen flowing from my lungs into my bloodstream, into the rest of my body.

As I breathe out, I visualize impurities from within my body being expelled into the air. As I exhale I emit an audible sigh. I let out a sound of deep relief as the air rushes out of my lungs. The sigh is meant to help fully push out the stale air from the bottom of my lungs. Sighing and yawning are the body's way of letting go of stress and tension.

I breathe in and out in this manner until I feel every muscle in my body relax. I very comfortably go limp.

When appropriate, I close my eyes, and do what Penny Pierce suggests when talking about softening awareness:[1] I close my eyes. I think of my brain as a muscle I can flex. Like any other muscle, I tighten it up, as though I was tightening my fist. Tighter. Tighter. Tighter. I tighten my brain as much as I can. I hold it that way until I almost feel myself shaking. Then I release it. I let it relax. I open my eyes and my mouth, and I drone some comfortable sound like a mantra.

I repeat this several times to "soften my awareness." Totally relaxing myself physically is a very important and necessary thing for me to do before I take the next step.

I Suspend My Assumptions and Judgments

While growing up I've heard those messages about intuition as something esoteric, something mystical, or something unpredictable. I totally and unequivocally discard those messages. I truly commit myself to the belief I can develop my skill of intuition. I view intuition as a way of knowing and I think it is as relevant a process for interpretation as any of my more physical senses—the way I know something when I see or hear or touch or taste or smell it.

This mind-set is very important because it takes me outside my normal box or my rules about the way I think.

Reflect back over the last several chapters, particularly my discussion of beliefs and perceptions. I know my mind is full of assumptions and beliefs that actually restrict the way I perceive and act. So the first step I must take to cultivate my intuition is to suspend my assumptions and judgments.

I came into adulthood with a host of judgmental "shoulds" and "should nots" and "dos" and "don'ts." They help me navigate in my physical and social worlds—they keep me safe and on an ethical and lawful course. But, as I've described in earlier chapters, these judgments can be very restrictive to me. At times, they sharply narrow my experiences.

---

[1] Penny Peirce, "The Silent Mind," *Article from Intuition Magazine 9/98.*

If I choose to develop my intuition, I must be willing to expand my experiences, or as our good friend and mentor, Nancy Nusser, calls it—"To Go Wide." I must free myself—at least in moments—from those judgmental strictures. This requires that I keep an open mind, a willingness to look at my positions and situations from totally different perspectives. I allow myself to think outside of my perceptual box.

For example, what about the most widely used definition of the word "intuition"? "The immediate knowing or learning of something without the conscious use of reasoning." What if I chose to challenge or broaden a part of the accepted definition? What if I ignore the part that suggests "without the conscious use of reasoning." After all, this is only someone's assumption. Does anyone really know for certain conscious reasoning must be eliminated from the equation in order to trigger my intuition? Why can I not come to an intuitive conclusion by consciously activating it with my reasoning ability?

My point is I seriously wonder if it is virtually impossible for me to develop my intuitive skill without first suspending my assumptions and my judgments.

I Become Consciously Present

What I mean by "becoming present" is I become even more conscious. I bring myself to a place where I become both the observer and the observed. I can best observe myself when I am focused. I allow my mind to do what it does. It wanders from this thought to the next. It notices this object and that object, this color and that color, this shape or that

shape. I am not invested in the past or the future. I am conscious about *being here now*. I take notice about what my mind is naturally drawn to think. When I am present, totally conscious, I am present with my thoughts.

Actually, I find the most difficult part of being present is simply a matter of thinking to do it. My mind is often so involved with my current thoughts and the processing of the data input entering into it through my objective and subconscious senses that I do not even consider being present.

So this component of Phase One serves a double purpose. When I am ready to "tune in" to my intuitive process, I stop to think to become present. A second benefit is each time I choose to become present, I am also practicing the art of being present. The more I am present, the more opportunities I have to grow and prosper as a human being.

I use these first three steps in Phase One (Relaxing My Mind and Body, Suspending My Judgments and Assumptions, and Becoming Consciously Present) as an intuition warm-up. I can do them anywhere—while I lie in bed after waking up in the morning, while I sit at my desk taking a break in the middle of the day, or while I relax after dinner in the evening.

This process opens my mind to my intuition. The more I take myself through the steps of this "tuning in" process, the quicker and easier it is for me to repeat them at a moment's notice.

Phase Two: "Tapping" into My Intuition

I Observe and Discern My Self-Talk

I do not try to clear my mind of self-talk, as I am prone to do while meditating. Instead, I notice what the self-talk is about and separate the wheat from the chaff. In other words, I notice what my mind is considering and whether it continues to focus on a specific image, thing, or thought.

Remember earlier in this book when I described my self-talk? I mentioned I am constantly talking to myself. In every split second, there is dialogue going on inside of my head. When I try to stop the dialogue, I find myself thinking about stopping the dialogue. That's really just more self-talk. When I try to stop thinking about stopping the dialogue, I then think about my attempt to stop thinking about stopping the dialogue. And so on. If I continued to try to stop my self-talk this way, I could drive myself a little crazy!

The strategy here is for me to allow my thoughts to naturally drift and wander. I am now ready to open myself up to experiencing my intuitive ability.

The Encarta World English Dictionary, North American Edition, defines the term "discern" to be able to distinguish between two or more things. For my purpose here, I regard "things" to be *thoughts*.

The discernment is meant to consciously observe my thoughts. When I am initiating this process I am purposely taking notice of where my mind is wandering. What am I unconsciously looking at, smelling, or even tasting or touching? Is there an unconscious meaning to this otherwise disconnected observation? Can I find intuitive meaning to this otherwise random observation? I continue to be present and aware of my thoughts.

I Ask Myself Questions and Observe My Answers

I purposefully ask questions about what I am observing in this moment.

When I am completely relaxed and present in the moment, I notice the random thoughts that begin popping in and out of my mind like little bursts of soap bubbles. I open my mind to them.

While noticing these random new thoughts, I keep myself alert for new ideas, new insights, and solutions to questions I've asked myself. When I notice an answer, I briefly focus on it. I accept my answers. I marvel at them and let them take me where they will.

What happens during these moments is very similar to what happens when I go to bed after unsuccessfully struggling to come up with an idea about something and then wake up with a brand-new idea fully blossomed in my mind.

I can choose to quickly ask questions that may or may not cause me to receive further information about that specific thought.

For example, as I am writing this chapter and I am thinking about how to phrase this exact sentence, my eyes wander from the monitor, and I notice my mind observing the wall to the left of my computer monitor. On the wall is a scattering of small frames containing Olympic pins I collected during the 1996 Olympics in Atlanta. To the right of the pins, I see a larger frame containing an array of political buttons I have collected over the years.

I notice that my state of mind swiftly changes from joyful interest in what I am writing about to a sense of disappointment and sadness. Now, this shift from concentrating on my writing to noticing a shift in my emotions occurs so quickly and is so subtle that under normal circumstances it would go unnoticed.

However, because I am intentionally being present in the moment, I am able to observe this change. I can choose to go back to writing, or I can choose to flow with the shift in emotions. I decided to explore the shift. In following the process I have been writing about I came to the conclusion I felt "sad" because the images of the display of pins and buttons triggered negative thoughts and feelings associated with disorder and being in disarray. In that moment I realized, for the first time, I was not consciously in control of my working environment.

So, you may wonder what this example has to do with "tuning in" to my intuition. First, it simply demonstrates the level of concentration and focus I am able to reach when I choose to be present in the moment. By observing the subtleties of my wandering thoughts I am in better position to also observe any intuitive responses my mind may offer.

And second, in keeping with one of my definitions of intuition that suggests intuition is a way of knowing—an unconscious assembling of sensory perceptions into meaningful patterns and predictions, and arriving at conclusions without having "analyzed" the facts—a true "gut feeling," I was actually analyzing the facts up until it occurred to me I was feeling "out of control." My mind then shifted to what I think was that "gut feeling." In this case it showed up as an insight that I may be out of control of my environment. As I do this I am listening to any answers that may enter my mind.

I Check for Any Noticeable Results

When I choose to act on my answers, I check to learn whether or not the answer or solution resulting from my action was beneficial. In the case of my example above I acted on it by (*a*) placing the pins and buttons in a more organized way into glass cases my wife had given to me a couple of years earlier; (*b*) I found now, when my eyes glanced to the left of my computer, I no longer felt sad. Instead a smile would come to my face, and I felt good.

I Practice, Practice, and Practice Some More

Over time, as I have developed my intuitive skills, I find myself intuiting at unexpected moments. I notice it when it happens. I accept my intuitive occurrences. I see them as my mind putting sensations and information together faster than I can think.

At first my intuition was not always correct. But over time, I have found myself becoming more accurate. I have learned to trust my intuition. The more I trust my intuition, the more it improves by leaps and bounds. As in all of the exercises I've described in this book, the final step in developing my intuitive sense is to practice cultivating it. Practice, practice, practice. No matter how much experts learn and report about how skills are developed, they never waiver from stressing the value of practice.

And throughout it all, I don't allow myself to be impatient— I am not afraid to fail at it. It's OK to fail. I learn lessons from failing. So I don't worry about it. I keep at it until I succeed.

I continue to cultivate my intuition. Since I have truly accepted it as a way of knowing something as valid as any of my other more physical senses, I have found myself successfully using my intuitive ability more and more.

Since I understood that I could choose to cultivate my intuition—once I truly accepted it as a way of knowing something as valid as any of my other more physical senses— I have found myself successfully and more consciously calling upon my intuitive ability over and over again.

A $10,000 Intuitive Hit

This wonderful experience just took place last night, and since I am still in the editing stage of this book, I decided it was too good a story not to include in this important chapter about what I think of as *Conscious Intuition*.

Here's the sequence of how this all played out.

For the past eleven years I have been involved in my Rotary Club's fundraiser, "An Affair To Remember." Each year we sell 275-350 tickets for $150.00. Each ticket allows two people to attend the event, partake of great food, drink the beverages of their choice, dance to the music of a live band, win door prizes, and be eligible to win one of three cash prizes: $500.00, $1,000.00, and the top cash prize of $10,000.00.

After all these years of purchasing tickets to support the event and the charities to which the profits are donated, I won the grand prize of $10,000.00. That alone is something to celebrate, but there is more to tell about this fortunate experience.

You see, a few nights before the event, I dreamt I won the $10,000.00. Now I suppose since I was the chairman of the event and also acted as one of two MCs, I was doing a lot of planning and thinking about the details of the fundraiser. It would make sense that my brain was filled with images about all of the particulars, even as I slept.

When I awoke the next morning the thought of winning the $10,000.00 was still in my brain. I thought this was a bit unusual since over the last ten years I never even considered winning; it just wasn't part of my thinking.

My day's agenda included arriving at the facility where we were going to hold the event to hang several banners and to help with some tasks that needed to be accomplished prior to the arrival of our guests.

As I was driving to the facility, appropriately named "My Special Place" in Woodstock, Georgia, I again thought about winning the $10,000.00.

Next, the thought crossed my mind, "What would I do if I won the top prize?" I remember quickly changing the words "*if I win*" to "*when I win*," a much more positive outlook. I didn't try to answer the question; I had arrived at the event facility, and it was time to take care of the tasks I was there to accomplish.

It was a few hours later, as I was driving home to clean up and change into my Tuxedo, when I again—albeit playfully—asked myself the question, "What would I do when I won the top prize?" The answer I heard in my mind was, "You will be in considerable trouble." I think my analytical mind took over as I wondered why I would I be in trouble.

Well, there were associated facts to consider. For instance, I was the chair of the event, I was the MC of the event, and I had a reputation in the community of being a guy who performs seemingly impossible memory and thought reading demonstrations and other amazing things with his mind. It was in that moment I knew what I had to do. I had to make it absolutely apparent that everything was on the up and up; I had to allow others to carry out the physical handling of the drawing. So I invited two prominent men whose credentials and ethics were above reproach. One person was the Cherokee County Sheriff, Roger Garrison, and the other was the State Court Judge of our county, Judge W. Allan Jordan.

I knew both of these gentlemen had purchased a ticket and were going to attend the function. Fortunately, both agreed to help. At the appropriate time I invited them to the bandstand where Rebecca Johnston, a local radio personality and also a member of our Rotary Club, would assist me in announcing the winners.

I should mention that whenever I conduct a raffle I make certain the very first ticket drawn from among all of the tickets becomes the winner of the grand prize—in this case, $10,000.00. My thinking is twofold. First the odds are so much greater and improbable when the first ticket drawn becomes the winner than if it was the second or third ticket drawn. And second, anyone whose ticket is drawn who does not win the top prize usually feels let down when they realize they no longer have an opportunity to win. So to avoid this and to keep the attendees in suspense I have a specific procedure I initiate.

I asked the sheriff to turn the tumbler containing several hundred ticket stubs, each identified with the contact information of the purchaser. I invited him to continue turning the tumbler and to stop at any time of his choosing and allow Judge Jordan to reach into the tumbler and without looking at the tumbler or the tickets, remove one ticket and place it into an envelope marked with the amount $10,000.00. The envelope was tacked onto a corkboard that stayed in sight at all times. This same routine was done with the second and third cash prizes, as well as with the top door prize, a 27-inch Magnavox flat screen television.

We then proceeded to give away all of the forty plus door

prizes. It took us about thirty minutes to accomplish this task. Now it was time to announce the winner of the top door prize, the TV, and then each of the three cash prizes. This was done in reverse order, the TV, the $500 cash, the $1,000 cash, and finally there was only one envelope with the $10,000 winning ticket stub inside still pinned to the corkboard.

I had asked Rebecca Johnston to read the names of each of the previous winners, and my intent was to read the name of the final winner of the $10,000.00 award.

I removed the last envelope from the corkboard, held it up to my forehead, and at that moment I again felt I had won. Speaking into the microphone I said, "I cannot announce the winner." I turned and handed the envelope to the sheriff, which he in turn opened. Sheriff Garrison showed the ticket stub to Rebecca and they both stared at me with looks of amazement. In that moment I absolutely knew that I had won. And sure enough, Rebecca announced the name of the winner of the $10,000.00 prize and it was indeed... Anton Zellman.

I was stunned! I guess I should not have been because my intuition was definitely working that day. After all, I did pay attention to it, and I did act on my intuitive premonition by becoming present whenever the thought of winning popped into my mind. I asked good questions and I observed the answers and acted on them as they came to me.

My wife, Lois, came running over towards me with great joy and excitement. She knew when she saw the look on my face that I had made a perfect hit. I had successfully predicted I would win.

In fact I was rather embarrassed that I had won, and I stood there somewhat in shock. For the rest of the evening almost everyone came up and genuinely showed their joy that we had won the grand prize.

Those are the facts as they happened. So what did any of this have to do with intuition? You may recall two of the points I suggest in my *Two Phase* process for *Conscious Intuition* are to check out the results and to practice, practice, and practice. Now looking back, I clearly see this was definitely an intuitive hit. This was one of those times I innately paid attention to whatever it was. Call it a hunch, a wish, an intuitive moment, or "peanut butter," the outcome was just as I had thought it would be. It paid off and provided me with additional fun and excitement along the way.

Was this a true conscious use of my intuition? I think so, but let me be clear about an important point. I don't believe I had any control or power over the outcome of that random drawing. What I do believe is I was able to pick up on the communications cues that were emanating from my mind, and I took this opportunity to be consciously involved with what I may have otherwise overlooked or simply dismissed as merely a coincidence.

Perhaps more and more, as I think about and act on these theories and concepts I have been talking about in this and other chapters of this book, they will become more naturally integrated with my daily mental activities. I look forward to many more *Conscious Intuitive* hits!

CHAPTER TEN

Creativity: Expanding My Mind

> Creativity involves breaking out of established patterns in order to look at things in a different way.
> —*Edward de Bono (b. 1933)*
> *Author and leading authority in the field of conceptual thinking*

Learning to make intuition a regular habit opened another wonderful door for me. I found myself becoming more creative, particularly in my ability to visualize, which is a very helpful skill for improving my memory. Developing my intuitive skill opened the door to new ideas, new ways of looking at things.

Use of my creativity is a key to expanding my mind.

To begin with, it is important to note creativity is a skill. It is not a genetically determined brain switch some have and some don't have. It is not innate. It is simply a skill anyone can develop.

More precisely, it is a thinking skill. Creativity is my thinking up new ways of seeing or doing things. It is combining thoughts and perceptions in ways I have not combined them before.

Inventors do it when they assemble materials into new useful objects. Artists do it when they combine images and colors in unique ways. Musicians do it when they meld sounds into melodies.

Developing My Creativity Skill

Clearly, the starting point in developing my creativity skill is to believe I can be creative.

The next step is to work through some simple exercises that give me opportunities to think and act creatively.

Let's try one. Do not turn the page upside down until you've tried this exercise. Consider the following fraction:

$$\frac{378}{126}$$

See if you can figure out three reasons for putting 378 on the top and 126 on the bottom. Think about it. What are some differences between the number (or numbers) on top and the number (or numbers) on the bottom?

Have you come up with some reasons? If you have, then turn the page upside down and look at some possible reasons. If you have difficulty finding three reasons, try for a few more moments, then look at the answer.

> The following solutions are three possible reasons why 378 is on top and 126 is on the bottom: (1) the number 378 is on top because it is a larger number than 126; (2) the number 378 is on top because it contains two odd numbers while the number 126 only contains one odd number; and (3) the number 378 is on top because when I spell out 3, 7, and 8 I find they are all five letter words, but when I spell out 1, 2, and 6 I find they are all three letter words—since five is greater than three, let's put the larger words on top. These are three suggested reasons. Are there more solutions?

Whatever you do, if you did not come up with three reasons, do not allow yourself to slip into the vicious belief cycle! After all, you probably didn't ride a bicycle perfectly or drive a car like a pro the first time you tried.

Before you read further than this paragraph, extend your practice with this exercise by making up some other fractions. Invent some similar fractions, each with their own solutions. This will help you expand your mind. It will exercise your creativity skill.

Then, when you feel you've done enough of that, try this next exercise. Again, do not turn the page upside down until you've finished the exercise.

Consider at least three ways in which these items are different from each other and then consider three ways all three items are alike. A bottle, a glass, and a bowl.

Think about it. Don't give up too quickly. When you are ready, turn the page upside down and read the solution.

> Three possible ways the items are different: (1) one is a bottle, another is glass, and the third is a bowl; (2) one contains beer, another contains water, and the third contains soup; and (3) one contains a cold liquid, another contains a liquid at room temperature, and the third contains a hot liquid. Three possible ways they are alike: (1) they are all containers; (2) they all contain liquids; and (3) they all are round (of course unless a square glass was used!). Are there other differences and similarities?

When I was solving the last exercise I saw mental pictures of the three containers as I was searching for solutions. That means I was visualizing. As represented in earlier chapters, I see visualizing as a very important tool in improving my memory.

But even more, I was *creating* pictures of the three objects. That's what visualization is. It's creating pictures. I was imagining three objects side by side I had never seen side by side before. I was combining three elements into a new whole. See, even visualizing the simplest of things gives me an opportunity to exercise my creativity skill!

But let's do more than just look for patterns—for differences and similarities. Let's do a bit of *inventing*. Once more, don't turn the page upside down until trying the exercise.

Come up with at least three things that can be done with each of these objects. Paper clips, a manila folder, and a rubber band.

> I can use a paper clip to bind several sheets of paper or unwind it and use the edge to clean out dirt between two tiles or link several of them together to make a necklace. I can use a manila folder to store important files or crumple it up to make packing material in a package or use it as a firm backing when mailing a picture in an envelope. I can wind a rubber band around several pencils to keep them together or I can put it around my wrist as a reminder to do something or I could put it over the top of my thumb, pull it back with my index finger, and then release it to shoot it at somebody.

Again, without consciously trying to I was creating pictures—mental images—as I was coming up with solutions.

Let's take it up a notch. Consider ways to use all three items *together*—the paper clips, the manila folder, and the rubber band. After creating a solution, turn the page upside down to compare lists.

Of course, solutions may vary. After all, there are no correct answers to exercises such as these, only different answers. This, indeed, is what creativity is all about!

As further practice, just as with the first exercise, the fraction exercise, come up with new variations of these last two exercises. Come up with other objects and look for their differences and similarities. Come up with other items and look for means with which they can be used, individually or together.

I find the more I do this, the easier it becomes. I add some fun to it. I choose some "crazy" combinations. How about a

Creativity: Expanding My Mind

circus clown, a red Porsche, and a globe of the earth? A fifth-grade teacher, a two-ton truck, and the Canadian army? The point is I have fun with these exercises. I strengthen my creativity skill more by having fun. My enjoyment reinforces my belief that I *do* have the capacity to create!

> I could open the folder slightly and set it up on the table like an upside-down V. Then I could stretch the rubber band between my index and forefinger of one hand (making a kind of sling shot), hold a paper clip against the edge of the rubber band, pull it back, and try to shoot it, trying to knock over the folder. I can picture myself doing this from different angles and different distances. I notice again this requires visualizing—I am *creating* mental pictures.

These three exercises are just the beginning. They merely help me to flex my creative muscle. Hopefully they begin to demonstrate we all have the capacity to be creative.

My Assumptions and My Creativity

My belief about how creative I am is not the only belief (assumption) influencing my creativity. Many times, I trap myself into not being creative because of the assumptions I make about what I am doing.

The problem of connecting the dots I described in chapter 6 is an excellent example. If I made assumptions I had to stay on the paper, I could not cut it up, and I could not fold it, I would have stifled my creative skill—my ability to come up with creative solutions to the problem.

Here's another example. Suppose I have twelve rods of equal length lying on the table in front of me. How could I arrange the twelve rods to form six squares all of the same size?

Before turning the page, play with this problem a bit. Use twelve new pencils or chopsticks or toothpicks—whatever is around can serve as twelve rods. Try arranging them into six squares of the same size. Go ahead. Try this exercise for a few moments.

How did it go? Successful? If the answer is "yes," skip over the next page, and let's move on.

CREATIVITY: EXPANDING MY MIND

If the answer is "no," take a moment to list assumptions that may be blocking the solution to the problem. If that doesn't help, then go on to the next page.

If you were unable to arrange the twelve rods so they formed six equally sized squares, don't get frustrated. Again, these exercises are for practice. The more of them you do the easier it will become. You are in the process of developing your creativity skill!

Most people will start by putting the twelve rods together in groups of four to form three equally sized squares, like so.

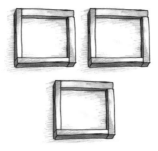

Some will place them in a fashion that forms four connected squares.

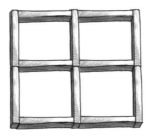

Then they'll stare at the four squares, and scratching their heads, they'll wonder how on earth they can rearrange them to make six squares! Some will say it's downright impossible.

The problem is they're trapped by an assumption. They started with twelve rods lying on a table, and so they assume they have to stay on the table in a two-dimensional space.

What if we break that assumption and instead assume that we can arrange the rods in a three-dimensional space?

Well, here we have it! The solution is to get a little glue and put the twelve rods together so they form a cube below:

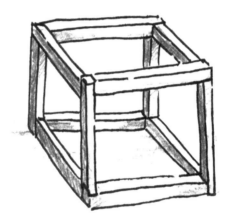

A cube has six sides, six squares, all of the same size. How about that? If you had difficulty getting to this solution, it was probably because the two-dimensional assumption got in your way. It stifled your ability to create.

Let's try another one. Look at the diagram below. How many square boxes can be seen in this drawing?

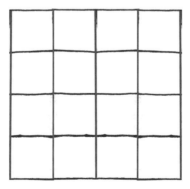

CREATIVITY: EXPANDING MY MIND

Sixteen? Nicely done. That is a logical conclusion. Four times four adds up to sixteen. Most people would agree there are sixteen square boxes.

But wait a moment! When I've used this diagram with audiences in my shows, I get all kinds of other responses to my question. Seventeen boxes. Twenty-two boxes. Twenty-five boxes. Twenty-six boxes. What's going on here?

Well, if I count the "cells" in this diagram, I certainly do come up with sixteen—sixteen square boxes. But, don't stop there. This entire discussion about creativity has been all about expanding my mind, *thinking outside the box*.

Look at the whole picture and imagine the cells are not there. What can be seen? That's right—*one larger square box*.

So, if I now look at my drawing with a more creative eye, I see I have a total of seventeen square boxes. But that's not all!

How about looking at the four cells in *each quad* of the diagram as *one square box*? Whoops! Now I can see up to twenty-one boxes. Get the picture? And don't forget to count the four-cell square in the center of the illustration.

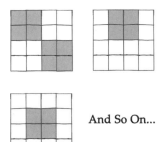

And So On...

To expand creative thinking and *before turning to the next page*, see how many more square boxes can be found in this illustration.

169

When looking at the various combinations of cells in the diagram, I can come up with a total of thirty square boxes.

Still cannot see all thirty boxes? Try looking for any four quads that contain nine cells.

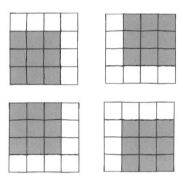

Once again, this exercise drives home a major point I have been making in this book. I am a creature of habit. I give power to my beliefs and my perceptions because I think I have to base everything that happens in my life on what I can see, taste, smell, touch, and hear. There's more going on out there!

It is very important for me to understand that to be creative, I must expand my mind. That's a big part of my learning how to read minds!

These last two examples along with the nine-dot example are abstract. But they do drive the point home. My beliefs and my assumptions *do* sometimes block my creativity.

Here's a problem a little less abstract. This is a modification of a problem used by Ernie Zelinski in his delightful book, *Thinking Big*. Ernie opines: "Suppose my family and I are living on a farm, and together we consume ten eggs every morning for breakfast.[2] But we haven't had chickens on our farm for

---

[2] Ernie J. Zelinski, Author of *The Joy of Thinking Big: Becoming a Genius in No Time Flat*, Published: March 1998 Ten Speed Press

over two years. We don't beg, borrow, steal, or buy eggs from anyone, and no one gives them to us. Where do we get our eggs?"

Consider this for a moment, before reading the next paragraph. Again, be aware of all assumptions.

Any assumptions suggesting my family and I were eating chicken eggs? The fact is, we all love to eat *duck* eggs, which is what we have every morning for breakfast.

If I didn't solve this, I probably was assuming the eggs were chicken eggs. I must continue to practice, practice, and practice some more. What all of these exercises are aimed at is for me to *expand* my creative thinking and to look *beyond* where I normally look for my answers and solutions.

Framing and Creativity

Psychologists suggest my "mental models" often bind my experience of the world. In other words, the collection of beliefs and assumptions I have about why things are the way they are can keep me from finding a different solution. These mental models give me *mental sets*—set ways of looking at things. Bound by my assumptions, I frame my view of a situation in a very specific way.

Developing my creativity skill requires me to *reframe* my view. Some people refer to this as "thinking outside the box." Others call it "divergent thinking." The point is, when I am faced with a situation in which I want to exercise my creativity skill, I try to look at the situation through a different window, through a different lens.

Years ago, a researcher at 3M Corporation in Minneapolis was experimenting with different kinds of adhesive materials. His goal was to develop a reliable tape with a very strong adhesive that could be used with such things as sealing packages. In other words, he was looking for a tape that would be an effective binder.

Along the way of his many trial adhesives, he came up with one on the back of a piece of paper that was just sticky enough to get the paper to adhere to a surface. However, it was not sticky enough to permanently hold to the surface. He could just peel it off. But then he could paste the piece of paper onto another surface.

Given his goal of developing a strong adhesive, he could have just stopped there. But he didn't. He *reframed* what he had. He thought how useful such a material might be to people who needed some temporary "stick-ons." On that day, Post-It® was born.

If I can consistently practice reframing, practice thinking outside the box, practice divergent thinking, and practice looking at a situation through a different window or lens then surely I will become more flexible in how I see and experience everything. I will further develop my creativity skill.

Three Books on a Shelf

Try this one on for size.[3] Suppose you had three journals next to each other on a bookshelf. Each volume is three inches thick and each has two covers. Now, suppose a bookworm was eating its way through the journals from the front cover of the first journal to the back cover of the third journal. How many inches does the worm travel?

---

[3] Inspired by Martin B. Ross, *Creativity and Creative Problem Solving* in the 1981 Annual Handbook for Group Facilitators (San Diego: Pfieffer and Company, 1981)

Before you jump to what might seem like an obvious conclusion, *picture* the journals on the shelf. Where's page one of the first journal? Where's the last page of the third journal? Take your time—think it through before you read the next two paragraphs below.

Most people would quickly jump to the conclusion the worm traveled nine inches, since each journal was three inches thick.

But wait a minute. Picture the journals on the bookshelf. Notice as you look at them, the back cover of the first journal is on the left side of the three journals and the front cover of the third journal is on the right side of the three journals.

This means the worm traveled only three inches—from the front cover of the first journal to the last cover of the third journal. This is clearly an example of a reframing of the third journal!

Let's try two more exercises. I won't give you the answer to the first problem—I will just let you develop answers on your own. First, suppose a carpenter ended up with a bunch of odd-sized pieces of scrap wood. He decides he'll just throw them out. But someone tells him, "No! Don't throw them out. There are all sorts of creative things we could do with those scrap pieces."

So take a moment right now and list at least ten things that could be done with those scraps of wood. While keeping this thought in mind: *This can be easily accomplished by using my capacity to be creative!*

That wasn't too difficult, was it? Now here is one more exercise that relies on an important key to developing your creativity skill—*having fun* while doing it! Add some silliness, some craziness to it. Reject the assumption that everything must have a serious purpose.

In the spirit of fun, I'm going to set up six outlandish conditions, then ask questions about them. Consider each condition and question one at a time. Use a fresh sheet of paper for each one. Write down as many things as come to mind. Come up with some crazy options. Draw pictures or diagrams if it helps. Above all, have fun with this exercise!

1. Suppose everyone had six fingers and no thumb on both hands. What changes would occur in the world and how would we live differently?
2. Suppose pollution has gotten so bad we all have to wear a plastic bubble around us with only our feet sticking out. How would the world be different? What would dating, courtship, and romance be like?
3. Suppose we had an extra set of eyes in the back of our head. How would that change things, especially our interpersonal relationships?
4. Suppose we only had two hours of sun per day every place in the world. How would that change the way we live?
5. Suppose we could teleport ourselves (like the people in *Star Trek*) anywhere in the world, instantaneously. How would that change the world and the way we live?
6. Suppose we could flap our wings and fly up to five thousand feet and up to ninety miles per hour. How would that change our lives, our fashions, and our interactions?

Well, I hope you had as much fun creating answers to these questions as I had making them up! Again, you and I are developing our creativity skills and expanding our minds.

A Note on My Brain and Creativity

Ever wonder exactly where creativity is located in the brain? The cerebral cortex is divided into two hemispheres—the right hemisphere and the left hemisphere. The two hemispheres are connected by a bundle of neurons known as the corpus callosum.

Over the last several years, some experts have speculated the right hemisphere is more involved in creativity and the left in more logical, analytic thinking. The truth as I understand it is brain research to this date has not yielded a precise, definitive answer. The most accepted answer these days is both hemispheres are involved, communicating with each other through the corpus callosum. This makes sense when I look at the evidence concerning each hemisphere.

The right hemisphere does appear to process more holistic processes—overall shapes of objects, the shape of words, and the information contained in the speaking of words strung together. The right hemisphere is the storehouse of multiple meanings of words and events, and more complex, figurative, and metaphorical visions of the world.

Meanwhile, the left hemisphere handles smaller, more precise meanings of things. The left hemisphere is more active in the literal understanding of language and analyses of small elements as opposed to complex combinations of many elements.

One expert refers to the right hemisphere as "context" and the left hemisphere as the "text."[4] The right hemisphere of the

---

[4] Robert Ornstein, *The Right Mind: Making Sense of the Hemispheres* (New York: Harcourt, Brace & Company, 1987), p.175.

brain is associated with the larger view, the left hemisphere with the details. Think back to what you did in the creativity exercises. You stepped back to look at situations from other angles, then combined smaller elements into different wholes. It makes sense to me that both the left and right hemispheres are involved in the creative process.

Whatever the case may be, all of the advice I gave to you in the third chapter about nourishing your brain is just as important to creativity as it is to memory.

CHAPTER ELEVEN

A Brief Pause: Recapping the Messages

> Man's mind stretched to a new idea never goes back to its original dimensions.
> *Oliver Wendell Holmes, Jr. (1884-1894)*
> *American author and physician*

At the start of this book, I promised to provide specific tools designed to help understand and sharpen my mental skills. I have presented key information about a variety of mental abilities along with a number of exercises designed to hone these abilities. I think those who really wanted to get the most out of this book will have taken, at minimum, several weeks to read it and to interact with the suggested exercises. So it seems appropriate to refresh your mind with a recap of the main thrust of particular messages described in each chapter.

Of course, I will continue my efforts to write this recap in the first person so as it is read, you will have the opportunity to either own or dismiss these messages as you choose.

Commitments and Benefits

In chapter 1, "Introduction: Why Read Minds?" I proffered that enhanced skills will free me from old mental scripts and programming, will point me down the path to self-discovery, and will lead me to achieve greater personal and professional success.

I also suggested, if I choose to commit to learning a variety of concepts and techniques, they will synergistically help me to improve my memory and to read the most important mind of all—*my own!*

Other important benefits derived from learning to improve my ability of memory and recall is I can also achieve tremendous improvement in my ability to concentrate, to experience perceptions based on more accurate sensory input, to communicate more effectively, and to make better choices and decisions.

Psychic Awareness

In chapter 2, "Mind to Mind: It's All about Communication," I asserted the first step to take if I want to learn to read the minds of others is to fully understand how to read my own mind and how it works.

Although I am typically doing it unconsciously, I am using my psychic awareness every day of my life. My memory, for example, is a psychic function of my mind I exercise each and every day of my life. My memory is a psychic awareness, a mental ability—that amazing ability to be able to store away information and access it at will. Thinking about it, I realize when I remember something, I am automatically reading my own mind!

Another point to consider is that memory in everyday life is rarely based on rote retention of detail. Instead, it relies heavily on remembering meaning, for example, the meaning of a passage, the meaning of a conversation, or the meaning of an event.

An important understanding I now have about memory ability is that, barring ill health at birth, I was born into this world with good, if not perfect, memory capabilities. In fact, again assuming good health in my brain, when I leave the planet, I will still have the capacity for perfect memory ability. I'm convinced it is possible to memorize and recall any amount of information I choose to remember, to do it at will and at any time in my life.

I/You Concept

Then in chapter 3, "The I/You Concept: Beyond My Self-Talk," I spoke of how strongly I believe one of the really magical qualities of my mind is I write my own life's scripts. I am the one who makes my choices for me. I bring to myself those things, those people, and those circumstances and experiences that I focus on and think about the most. *My choices* shape my experiences.

I believe self-talk is one of the most powerful functions of my mind. I place it right up there with visualization and imagination. It is a magical tool and I must use it wisely.

Simply put, when I talk about my feelings or actions in the *second* person, that is to say when I use the word "you" when it would be more appropriate to use the word "I," it means I *am not* taking ownership of those feelings or actions. When I talk about my feelings or actions in the *first* person, I *am* taking ownership of my feelings and my actions.

Notice the difference? Second-person speaking (or thinking) puts my feelings and actions "out there," away from myself, not part of me—no ownership.

When I speak (or think) in the first person, my feelings and actions are mine, part of me—I own them.

All those around me, then and now, are models for who I am. I have been and am being modeled by all of the programming passed down to me from my ancestors, by the institutions I attend, by the books I read, by movies and television programs I view, by the radio programs I hear, and even by the music to which I listen.

If I am only speaking in second person, I am camouflaging who and what I am and can be because I feel vulnerable. I am shutting out 90 percent of who I can become by simply being like everyone else.

Human Brain

In chapter 4, "My Brain: The Nuts and Bolts of My Memory," I presented a brief description of how science describes how the brain works. I expressed that long-term memory takes place in the cerebral cortex, the highly developed, thinking part of the brain. This is particularly important because it is in the cerebral cortex that the mental processes having to do with thinking, perceiving, listening, and creating take place—all of which, as I described in subsequent chapters, directly influence my ability to store and remember things.

I also described how the human brain is made up of complexly interconnected nerve cells, called neurons. And I talked about neurotransmitters, the chemicals that affect communication among the neurons. The proper levels of those neurotransmitters are affected by nutrition, exercise, my emotional state, and how much I stimulate my brain.

The most important point to remember from chapter 4 relevant to improving my memory is how to keep my brain healthy. I need the right balance of protein, complex carbohydrates, simple carbohydrates, and fats to keep me mentally alert. I need the proper amount of aerobic exercise to improve the quality of my mental functioning. I need to find ways to reduce the amount of stress in my life, because stress redistributes blood away from my brain. Finally, I can use my brain to stimulate my brain, to exercise it like a muscle, in order to keep my brain active and growing.

Neuro-Linguistic Programming (NLP)

In chapter 5, "NLP: A Window to My Thinking," I introduced the concept of Neuro-Linguistic Programming (NLP), which stems from the notion that my experience of things is based on my thinking. Again, I come back to the cerebral cortex.

NLP helps me understand the way my senses are connected to my neurological processes. Knowing about those connections helps me become more aware of the kinds of "programming" I have developed over the years. That programming directly affects the choices I make. The choices I make directly affect my ability to remember.

Using NLP, I described how people prefer one or a combination of three different thinking processes related to their senses: visual, auditory, and kinesthetic. I then demonstrated how those thinking processes are linked to memory, and how I use that knowledge to improve my memory.

Beliefs and Assumptions

In chapter 6, "Beliefs: I Do What I Believe I Can Do," I discussed the central importance of the beliefs and assumptions I make when I think. In particular, I pointed out the connection between my beliefs and my actions.

Becoming aware of how my beliefs filter interpretations of my experiences as those experiences are registered in my brain is an important step to improving any of my mental skills. Many of my beliefs stifle me in far more situations than I may have previously realized.

The other concept besides *belief* that emerges as a cornerstone of these first several chapters is the concept of *choice*.

Every action I take is a choice. Even in situations where I think I have no choice, I do, in fact, have a choice.

My beliefs and my assumptions *structure* the window through which I see my world. If I believe I am not capable of achieving something, then I won't choose to take actions that would lead me to achieve it.

If I choose to believe I will never be able to remember anything, chances are I won't choose to learn how to improve my memory.

Examining my choices to uncover and challenge my beliefs can feel very risky. It's so much easier to stay in my comfort zone. But if I want to expand my mind, if I want to grow, I have to take some risks.

Using a few playful exercises, I demonstrated the powerful influence assumptions have on my thinking. I stressed the importance of consistently challenging those assumptions every time I catch myself in any kind of I-can't-do-it self-talk.

I then described two elaborate memory exercises, along with an acronym for recalling the exercise, to help me remember names that make use of my visual, verbal, and kinesthetic memory.

In the first memory exercise, I described my three-minute technique for remembering names. I call it *Take Three,* because it is a simple exercise I can repeat three times in three minutes as I introduce three people to each other three times. The exercise trains me to use all three types of memory: *visual, verbal,* and *kinesthetic* in a systematic way.

The acronym I suggested for recalling the picture-association process is **AIR**—**A**ttention! **I**nterest! **R**epeat! Consciously pay *attention* and really listen when a person's name is first spoken. Be *interested* in the person with whom you are speaking. And *repeat* the person's name as you mentally create a silly picture that will trigger the name of this person when you next meet.

This concept is made clear in the second mnemonic technique I described for remembering names. The main component is to create a silly or zany image for the person whose name you want to store away and recall. If I have a reference in my mind for that name then I use it to create my picture. If I do not have a reference, then I create pictures out of the syllables or "sound-alike" words of a person's name.

Once I have created my picture for the person's name, I want to link or associate it. By this I mean I want to mentally have my picture interact, in a bizarre, absurd, or funny way, with some part of the person's head or face.

What We See

In chapter 7, "Perception: I See What I Think I See," I extended the discussion of beliefs and assumptions to describing how they influence the way I perceive my world. I cited examples of research that demonstrate how powerfully beliefs and assumptions influence what I see. I demonstrated that influence with two exercises to illustrate how the context of whatever I am looking at further determines what I see.

I finished the chapter by doing a simple visualization exercise. Visualization is a skill immensely helpful to me in improving my memory.

A BRIEF PAUSE: RECAPPING THE MESSAGES

What We Hear

In chapter 8, "Listening: I Hear What I Want to Hear," I moved to another sensory process very important to the effectiveness of my memory, listening. I stressed how active and effective listening is hard work. It requires me to carefully concentrate. It calls for me to maintain a clear focus.

I then reviewed some steps I use—some guidelines—for learning how to listen more effectively.

These include overcoming my tendency to push my own agenda and to *stop talking* so I can be open to receiving what others have to say; *paying attention* to what the other person is saying and not allowing myself to be distracted or drift off into unrelated self-talk; *observe nonverbal messages*—noticing the movements of the speaker's eyes, the posture of the body, and gestures; *listening objectively* to what the other person is saying without getting sidetracked by my beliefs and assumptions; *listening analytically*—identifying themes and key ideas, and organizing the information I am hearing; and *listening with empathy*—trying to feel the world as the speaker is feeling it. These active listening techniques are very important to remembering. They help me truly hear what it is I am listening to.

Intuition—My Other Sense

In chapter 9, "Intuition: My Other Sense," I discussed still another form of perception: intuition. At any given moment, I see, hear, feel, taste, and smell much more than I realize. Intuition adds another dimension to all the information I absorb every day through my other senses.

I described a *two-phase* process I use to cultivate and practice my intuition.

I initiate Phase One consisting of the following three actions in preparation for Phase Two:

1. I relax my mind and my body.
2. I suspend my assumptions and judgments—the "rules" that keep me from "thinking outside the box."
3. I become consciously present. I actively initiate my mind to be present, observing, and opening myself to intuitive experiences.

Now I am ready to begin Phase Two, which is designed to cultivate and exercise my innate power of intuition.

- I observe and discern my self-talk.
- I mentally ask questions.
- I observe and discern my answers.
- I check any noticeable results.
- I practice, practice, and practice some more.

My intuition opens the door to my creativity and to my self-development.

Visualize, Imagine, and Create

In chapter 10, "Creativity: Expanding My Mind," I focused on several related skills and exercises that help me to develop, envision, and manifest positive results for the goals I choose to achieve in my life. I can enhance my mental skills of *creativity, visualization, and imagination*. I can keep my mind open and flexible as I perceive and listen to another person.

I acknowledge the hazard of impeding myself from developing these skills by believing I am not creative or I cannot visualize or imagine. I know I *am creative*, and I understand my beliefs and assumptions can stifle my creative skill in other ways.

Reframing is yet another technique I can use to help me be more creative. Instead of viewing failure as bad, I realize I can look at failure as an opportunity to learn and to grow. That's

A Brief Pause: Recapping the Messages

what successful people do. If I can consistently practice reframing, practice thinking outside the box, practice divergent thinking, and practice looking at a situation through a different window or lens then surely I will become more flexible in how I see and experience everything.

Finally, I also added information in chapter 10 about how my brain is involved in creativity. I explained the cerebral cortex is divided into two hemispheres, the right hemisphere and the left hemisphere. The two hemispheres are connected by a bundle of neurons known as the corpus callosum.

The right hemisphere does appear to process more holistic processes—overall shapes of objects, the shape of words, and the information contained in the speaking of words strung together. The right hemisphere is the storehouse of multiple meanings of words and events, and more complex, figurative, and metaphorical visions of the world.

Whatever the case may be, all of the recommendations I provided in the third chapter about nourishing the brain are just as important to the maximum use of my creativity as it is to memory.

OK, I think I have adequately provided the tools I promised in the first chapter. I have related in the previous ten chapters what I believe to be solid information along with my personal viewpoints on the brain, NLP, perception, listening, intuition, creativity, beliefs, assumptions, choice, and risk. I chose these particular topics because I wanted to provide you with an ever-expanding mind-set. I wish for you to be willing to experiment and to challenge yourself to "go wide" in your thinking.

All of these tools when understood and practiced as a synergistic endeavor may very well set the stage for honing the ability to conscious and accurate reading of each others' minds.

CHAPTER TWELVE

Reading My Own Mind: I Am a Living Example

> We choose our joys and sorrows long before we experience them.
>
> —*Kahlil Gibran (1883-1931)*
> *Poet, philosopher, and artist*

I began this book with the notion that the information and exercises I express are, collectively, the first step to understanding how to read minds. In the next two chapters I will, once again, provide an opportunity to practice doing just that—read minds. However, before I do, I want to relate a few examples of how I have utilized some of these skills to read my own mind. Remember, I have stated I am a living example of this ongoing process.

Fortunately, I am diligent about being conscious of and attempting to understand the beliefs and perceptions that are part of the fabric of who I currently am. Knowing what motivates me to think and behave as I do enables me to make new choices. Conscious choices can help me shift my thoughts, to achieve a healthier and rewarding life.

It seems appropriate to me to mention that my purpose for revealing so many of my self-defeating habits along with those that give me successful results is to emphasize my "will"ingness to be conscious. Looking back now, I can clearly see how I unconsciously called upon my mental skills to get me through many of my life's situations and challenges. On the next few pages I'm going to catalog the "mental tools" I believe I used in each situation.

So it all makes sense, I will list each skill beneath a topic headline that relates back to specific information I have outlined in various chapters of this book. Please keep in mind each instance I list is not necessarily connected directly to the previous one. My purpose here is to distinguish and understand the relationship of each challenge to the specific skills I've worked so conscientiously to enhance. I believe I've accomplished a lot, but of course, I know I still have a long way to go.

Motivated By Crisis

Sometimes it seems as though there is nothing like a crisis to motivate me to action, like the one I experienced in July of 1994. My doctor told me I had cancer in my bladder. Fortunately, because I paid attention to my symptoms and took immediate action, I caught the cancer in its early stages, and my doctor used his expertise to surgically remove it before it could cause the loss of my bladder, or worse.

Talk about sensing modalities and memories! I can clearly see, hear, and feel many of the situations associated with this period in my life. Although I took it very seriously, it's interesting to me (and I hope to you) how I was able to find and use my wit and sense of humor to help get me through it all.

For instance, from the moment I heard the word "cancer," I seemed to be in a time warp. Everything was happening very fast. I noticed my symptom (blood in my urine) on a Friday night. On Saturday morning, I called to make an appointment with a urologist, Dr. Kenneth Rutledge. He examined and interviewed me on Monday morning. On Tuesday and Wednesday, I subjected my body to the appropriate battery of tests. On Thursday morning I was on the operating table.

During the Monday interview I asked Dr. Rutledge: "Doctor, how long have you been performing this procedure?" (Hey, I've learned a little something while attending 190 medical conferences over the years)

"About fourteen years," he replied.

"Well, that worries me," I said.

"Why is that?" asked Dr. Rutledge.

"I'm sure you must be very good at your job," I answered, "however, I'm concerned that, having performed so many procedures of this type over fourteen years, by now, you may be doing it like a robot. You see, we don't have much time to get to know each other between now and when you operate. But I want you to know if we did have the time and you had a chance to get to know me, well, I'm sure you would begin to love me. So I'm requesting you love me as you perform this procedure."

I wanted and got his attention! He smiled a little but didn't say anything more.

Then it was Thursday. I was lying on the table, and the anesthesiologist was giving me the anesthesia. Just as I was about to drift off to sleep I looked into the doctor's eyes. "Don't forget to love meeeeeeee," I said, as I drifted off to sleep.

I would have liked to have heard what the nurses had to say, given the fact the operation was being performed as a cystoscopy through my . . . well, you know what I mean. And, of course, the nurses were not privy to my first conversation with the doctor.

Sometime later I awoke. There was the doctor looking into my eyes.

"Anton," he said, "I loved you, the surgery went well, and you're going to be fine."

Meditation and Visualization

Following the operation, due to a variety of circumstances, I took eighteen months off from work to rest, collect my thoughts, and recuperate.

At first, I was very concerned about finances and the loss of my business contacts. After all, I had worked long and hard to build up our cash reserves. I could see my capital flowing out without any coming in. Also, I knew from experience my best marketing device was to be out there working, to be seen presenting to many people. I went through a couple of weeks of playing "poor me." But, I then decided to start using the ideas I had been cultivating for so long.

I meditated a lot. I opened up to new possibilities. I realized I had to tap into my creativity and shift my thinking if I wanted to receive a positive result from this experience. So I decided to view my time off as an opportunity rather than a threat.

I began to view it as an opportunity to spend time enjoying my family and friends, an opportunity to engage in some self-discovery. I saw it as a way to enjoy a year or two of my retirement, just a few years early.

I enjoyed precious time with my wife, Lois, who so lovingly took care of me during my convalescence. I spent time with my children in Ohio. I was available to be with my daughter, Tricia, when she delivered her first baby, our first grandchild, Jessica Nicole. I devised a new marketing plan to lease my services to corporations. I spent a lot of my time participating in community activities and projects.

A Conscious Use of My Belief System

In March 1996, I went back to work, speaking and presenting. I negotiated two great contracts with new clients. I felt terrific! Income was once again flowing in. Life was good.

Then in September 1997, I discovered I had another health crisis. I experienced much shortness of breath, mild pains in my chest, and some numbness in my left arm.

Enter into my life heart specialist and surgeon, Dr. Gregory Simone, who performed an angiogram and other tests to find out what was going on. He informed me I had serious blockage in the two main arteries to my heart, and my cholesterol level was 294 and climbing. He told me I had two choices: surgery or a lifestyle change—Duh!

For a guy who was healthy for most of his life and never really had a family doctor other than pediatricians for the kids and gynecologists for my wife, I could now claim I had a team of great doctors looking after me.

It was time once again to consciously tap into a positive part of my creativity and belief system. For the next fourteen months I dedicated myself to doing all the right things in order to become healthy and to avoid going through a heart attack or another surgery. After all, it made no sense to me to survive cancer only to die of a heart attack.

Well, to make a long story short, I became the perfect patient. In three months' time, I had my total cholesterol level down to 141. And all of my other numbers were also on target. I did all the correct things to maintain a healthy lifestyle. I meditated frequently. I exercised. I followed a near-no-fat diet. And yes, I faithfully took my medications every day.

Choice Originates from a Belief

I also used this time to sharpen my own skills at what I do for a living. I created new ideas and practiced my presentations.

Many people who see and hear me speak ask me how I learned to deliver my talks with so much confidence, sincerity, and enthusiasm. My answer is always the same: preparation, preparation, preparation, and practice, practice, practice.

Even today, after twenty-nine years of public speaking I still script every presentation I deliver, in great detail, and I practice. My primary reason is I feel safe when I am well prepared. It increases my level of confidence. The practice helps me to recall the cadence and timing of my delivery.

Also, I have an unyielding, longtime commitment to giving every audience a thousand percent of my energy, my enthusiasm, my knowledge, and my love. Remember, a commitment is a choice. A choice originates from a belief or an assumption.

Creative Insight

About five thousand presentations ago, I came to realize I had a huge obligation to each and every audience. After all, I understood the members of each audience were taking their valuable time to listen to what I have to say, and to view the mind demonstrations I was performing. I also realized, in a sense, no matter what the event, "it was their night out," and they were seeking some distraction from their daily routines and life's many challenges.

I further recognized it was my job to give them the very best presentation, talk, or show, of which I was capable. To accomplish this, I wanted to be certain my conversation with my audience was educational, as well as entertaining. I decided I also wanted to provide them with amazement, fun, and joy.

I began to understand that to accomplish this it must be my night out as well. I must also enjoy every moment of my time onstage or on the platform. If not, then I may as well give up speaking and performing for my living and go back to being a sales representative. That's not to suggest being a sales representative was such a bad thing. I simply do not have the same passion for sales as I do for teaching, speaking, and performing.

That's the way I've approached every engagement during my career as a public speaker, as an "edutainer," and as a "perceptionist." I know what you're thinking, "What the heck is a perceptionist?" Well, frankly, it's a fifty-dollar title I invented during my first year (1973) as a performing mentalist. Another example of utilizing creativity is I also coined the terms "edutainer" and "edutainment" that same year.

Drawing upon My Enhanced Mind Skills

In keeping with the theme of this chapter, "I Am a Living Example," I want to describe another significant episode in my life. It more clearly demonstrates my conscious and unconscious use of the many mind skill enhancements, which I've described in this book. The story is about my year as president of my local Rotary Club.

In 1995, I was invited by my club members to "move through the chairs" and become president of the club for the Rotary year 1997-1998.

I thought long and hard before I accepted. This would be the first time in my life I ever took the helm for anything except to provide for my family and to take care of my business. I must admit I was very anxious and had a lot of self-doubt about my ability to meet this huge challenge.

But meet it I did. I chose to suck in my fear and overcome my doubts about how well I could do. I accepted the commitment to lead our club. You can bet I intended to treat every weekly Rotary Club meeting and each monthly board meeting I was to lead with the same enthusiasm and commitment as I would give to a paid engagement.

To put this into proper context, it is important for me to explain that a Rotary year begins in July and ends in June of the following year. Rotarians are committed to attend a Rotary meeting fifty weeks a year. Rotary Clubs can be found in more than 29,000 cities, towns, and villages in 163 countries around the world. So if I were to miss a meeting with my home club while I'm traveling, all it takes to make it up is a commitment to attend a meeting at another nearby club in the city to which I had traveled. Modern technology allows me to go to the web site, *www.rotary.org*, to locate the nearest club.

My first challenge as president was to be sure every meeting was planned in advance. I also made certain there was someone in place to fill in for me when I traveled—since I was scheduled to make eighteen business trips during that twelve-month period.

It would be a challenge for the membership as well, because as far as I know, I was the first traveling president in the sixty-year history of the club. So planning was paramount to making certain my club ran efficiently. And boy, did I plan—after all, creating, planning, and directing a production is a large part of my occupation. In fact, my wife likes to laughingly say to friends: "Anton can make a huge production out of anything."

I spent considerable time scripting every Rotary meeting as though it was a major production. This required that I use all of my mental abilities of creativity, concentration, and visualization.

For example, I invited eleven past presidents of our club to fill in for me while I traveled to engagements in other cities. I gave a detailed weekly script to each past president, so all they had to do was follow the script.

Beliefs and Assumptions

Despite all of my strategizing and planning, I soon learned my body and mind were about to provide me with larger challenges.

In November 1997, during the first half of my year as president of my Rotary Club, I experienced my second bout with bladder cancer. Once again, I had the cancer removed surgically. However, this time it was also necessary to remove a small portion of my prostate in the process.

It had been almost three years since my first cancer operation. I was caught off guard hearing this news. After all, I had faithfully been going in for my checkups every three months, living a life of proper nutrition and exercise, and I was experiencing a minimal amount of stress. I really thought I had beaten the ferocious disease after the cancer was removed in July of 1994. In addition to mentally handling my disappointment, I experienced a great loss of focus and energy for at least six months, both from the operation and the medications.

I Am Always Using My Willpower: Either I Will or I Will Not

I recall lying in my bed in the hospital, thinking about how diligently I had worked for the past fourteen months to keep myself healthy. I thought about how hard I worked so I could avoid experiencing an angioplasty procedure. And for what? Here I was, once again, fighting cancer.

It seemed as though I could not stop thinking about all the tasty food I had given up. Another issue was the extra effort it took for my sweet wife, Lois, to accommodate my new eating habits. So I once again tapped, perhaps somewhat unconsciously, into my belief system and made a new choice.

I "willfully" chose to "give in a little." To go easy on myself, and to occasionally enjoy some foods (meat, sweets, breads, etc.) for which I so dearly yearned. I also chose to allow myself to drink a little wine with dinner. After all, I could have died from the cancer. What if it came back again? Why should I choose to disallow myself from enjoying a few pleasures in life? Why not anesthetize myself through this huge disappointment?

Whoops! This is not as innocent as it may sound. I now realize something else was operating here. In addition to all my other talents, I also have what has been identified as "a compulsive-addictive personality." In short, my history has been that I overindulge in what I feel is pleasurable to me. I especially do this during those moments when I do not want to face the situation at hand. If I am not vigilant, I can eat too much food, drink too much alcohol, or smoke too many cigarettes, and so forth.

So here I was, in the middle of struggling with my health crisis, I was also going to have to do battle with some deep-rooted, destructive habits.

Now, the good news is I had not smoked for thirty-one years, and I still do not smoke. Also, I had not had a drink of alcohol for almost fifteen years and as previously mentioned I had been sticking to a low-fat, nutritious diet for about fourteen months.

It became apparent to me that my choice to "give in a little" was setting me up for a longer period of convalescence. In turn, it would make it more difficult for me to achieve my goal to be as good a Rotary Club president as I could possibly be. It also would make it more difficult for me to remain healthy so I could enjoy many years of retirement, which seemed to be just around the corner. Without a doubt I was battling some heavy, negative programming.

In chapter 6 on "Beliefs: I Do What I Believe I Can Do," I said my programming includes many different beliefs that can and will bring me either positive or negative results. I called on various parts of my belief system as I went through this period of health, business, and personal challenges. After a period of time, I consciously chose to emphasize the "will" in my willpower in order to overcome the negativity permeating my thoughts. I drove myself with my belief that I could meet any challenge.

I've come to realize I am always using my "willpower." It's not a matter of learning to implement my "willpower" but instead, it's a matter of making a choice. Every time I assert my power of choice I am using my "willpower." With every decision I make I either decide I "will" do something or I "will not" do something. Either I "will" give in to my habit of overindulging in food, alcohol, and other gratifications, or I "will not" give in to overindulging in food, alcohol, and other gratifications.

As I write this chapter, I am pleased to report I've been "willfully" eating differently, I have lost a good deal of weight, and am managing to maintain the weight loss. I'm "willfully" taking all of my medications, vitamins, and supplements every day. My cholesterol numbers are still on target with an ongoing range of 140-176.

However, even now, I still find myself battling against my "willfully," albeit occasional, indulging in drinking alcohol and at times to excess. Nor am I exercising nearly enough. The good news is I am aware I need help in this area of my life. So for almost three years now I've met with a psychologist three to four times a month. At each session I am discovering more about myself, why I think as I do, and bit by bit, I'm learning how to deal with the part of me that easily gives in to my compulsive-addictive personality.

Using Mnemonics to Organize and Recall

Because I desired to provide the Rotary membership with a top-notch meeting every week, I utilized mnemonics to organize and recall what I needed to communicate at each meeting. Even though I can be somewhat anal about being prepared and I fully script my talks, I seldom, if ever, read from my notes. I think if I am to be knowledgeable and believable to my audience, then I should speak as though I thoroughly know my topic. I don't think I ever missed a beat.

On another level, I reached into my long-term memory to recall similar experiences where I was able to overcome difficult situations, and I was able to overcome my fears. I remembered that I have a long history of overcoming adversity.

I recalled hearing the voice of Norman Vincent Peale saying, "The human mind does not create problems—it only creates projects to keep it busy. And it would not create a project it was not capable of successfully achieving."

Expectations Can Often Lead to Disappointment

I decided to consciously take a serious look at the influences and context of my perception of this second cancer episode in my life. I came to realize I had set myself up for the disappointment I experienced when it happened. I was clearly told after my first operation that there was a fifty-fifty chance the cancer would show up again. I chose to hear what was said to me, as "I will not have a relapse."

In fact, during my meditations I used my powers of imagination and visualization to see my bladder free of cancer. I would visualize a soft chalkboard eraser wiping clean the lining of my bladder. I firmly believed I was doing something positive to help my body to remain free of cancer. All of this added up to having an expectation of cancer not returning.

Now, make no mistake about it. I did receive positive benefits from my meditations and visualization exercises. There is no doubt in my mind that I was able to handle many situations because I was not consumed by worry and fear. I felt more in control, and when I am in control, I am not filled with worry and fear of the unknown.

However, that being said, how long do I have to be on this planet before I get the message that expectations bring disappointment? The fact of the matter is a long time ago I chose to smoke, and I smoked a lot. My body could not totally deal with the poisons I had inhaled. Everything I hear from urologists and oncologists suggests that the only consistent connection they can find between men and cancer of the bladder is smoking. So it was an earlier "willful" choice in my life that caused the cancer in my bladder.

Perception

I also realized that a perception I had incorporated into my habit system as a child was still playing itself out as an adult. Whenever I had to deal with an uncomfortable situation as a child, I escaped into my fantasies and anesthetized myself with stuff that gave me pleasure, such as eating lots and lots of candy. As an adult, I shifted to using substances like alcohol and large quantities of food to help me hide from my situation. Eventually I realized this certainly was not a good way to help my body to heal and grow healthy.

Fortunately, by looking at these perceptions, I was able to make new choices to counter them during this health-crisis period in my life. It seems appropriate to me to mention my reasoning for revealing so many of my negative beliefs and perceptions.

Recall my saying at the outset my overall intent in writing this book was to understand more about how I think and behave. To line up all of the concepts, programs, scripts, and experiences that formed my beliefs, opinions, and behaviors. In every sense of the term—to "read my own mind." I do not claim to be able to live out, at all times, every positive concept I have written about on these pages. But, as I have stated, I am a work in progress. And to the degree that I am able to see the errors, mistakes, and poor choices I make will I be able to work through them and achieve the success in becoming a more balanced and loving person.

Listening

During my convalescence, it was imperative for me to practice the six steps to effective listening, which I spoke about in chapter 8 (see page 129). For instance, I recall using the third step—observe nonverbal messages—to a great advantage. As I mentioned, concentration and focus were a real effort for me. Once I arrived at our Rotary meeting place, I found it difficult to think about carrying out all the details of my office, conducting the meeting, and answering all of the questions the members asked of me when they arrived. So, although I had difficulty concentrating on every word they spoke, I was able to read a lot of what they wanted by observing their nonverbal cues. I was able to take in more accurate information and remember it more effectively until I was able to write down their requests.

In the End, I Was Successful

Under my leadership and the active participation of the club members, our Rotary Club won the highest district award as Club of the Year in the medium-size club category.

This turbulent period was also a period of personal awards as well. My Rotary Club honored me with The Rotarian of the Year award. I was honored by the Georgia State House of Representatives with a Commendation (H.R. No. 385) for my services as a leading Rotarian of my club and for active services to my community. As an added treat, my peers in the International Psychic Entertainers Association, as represented by a board of directors, awarded me the prestigious Joseph Dunninger Award for Excellence and Professionalism in the Performance of Mentalism.

I realize I've been tooting my own horn a lot in this chapter. I did experience a great amount of joy in attaining these personal achievements—however, my intent in reporting them is not for personal aggrandizement. I mean for them to illustrate that even in the most troubling of times it was possible for me to tap into a variety of mental skills and techniques (sometimes even remarkable skills) to deal with circumstances that might otherwise have overwhelmed me.

My sincere wish is that those who read this book will be triggered to action by the stories and anecdotes I have been sharing, to consciously connect with their own experiences and challenges and to be inspired to overcome those challenges. To clearly know that through the understanding and making use of the workings (reading) of his or her own mind, everything is possible.

Keep at it. This stuff really does work!

So now let me give you an opportunity to toot your own horn!

CHAPTER THIRTEEN

Understanding and Reading Your Own Mind:

All It Takes Is Practice

> Only as you do know yourself can your brain serve you as a sharp and efficient tool. Know your own failings, passions, and prejudices so you can separate them from what you see.
> —Bernard M. Baruch (1870-1965)
> *American financier and advisor to six presidents*

Recall my saying near the beginning of this book that I must be able to read my own mind before I can read the minds of others. Throughout this book, I've provided many insights and techniques to do just that.

Now I'm going to offer five simple exercises to tie it all together. Don't rush through this chapter. Take all the time needed to complete one exercise before going on to the next, because each exercise builds on the one before it.

By the time you go through all of them, you will know your own mind a whole lot better. And you will be better prepared to read the minds of others.

Also, I am going to switch my language to second person "you" because I will be speaking directly to *you* and asking *you* to do specific tasks. If *you* choose to, feel free to substitute "I" for "you" so *you* can truly own these exercises.

Rising Above Flatland

Before you begin the five exercises, let me set the stage by telling you a story about an imaginary place called "Flatland."

I Read Minds—And So Do You!

I first heard about this story from my friend Arnie Dahlke who told me how profoundly it influenced his life. I have been equally touched in a positive way, so I'd like you to look at this story as a metaphor for yourself as you practice reading your own mind.

Flatland is a two-dimensional world, where creatures only have length and width, but no depth. Instead of the cubes, spheres, and pyramids we see in our world, Flatland inhabitants are squares, circles, and triangles. A square by the name of *A. Square* is the narrator of the book. He describes life in his flat world, about its politics, about sex among consenting triangles, and about many other local customs. But, more importantly, the two-dimensional Flatlanders are unaware of the third dimension!

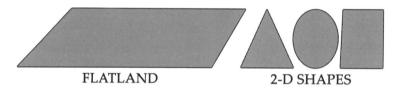

FLATLAND   2-D SHAPES

One day, a sphere approached this two-dimensional world. Being a curious creature, he decided to visit the Flatlanders. But since Flatland has only length and width, they saw him as a circle in the place where he intersected the plane of their world.

To see how this happened, picture a sphere coming up through a piece of paper. When it first touches the paper, it appears as a dot. As it continues to pass upward through the paper, it becomes a circle that grows larger until the widest part of the circle—its "equator"—passes through. Then, it shrinks until it becomes a dot again. And then it disappears as it continues upward, moving above the paper.

From their two-dimensional point of view, the Flatlanders saw

this visitor change size and even become a dot, only to disappear and then reappear somewhere else in Flatland as it penetrated their world in another place.

The sphere explained to the Flatlanders what was happening. He told them about the third dimension and tried demonstrating it by moving in and out of their two-dimensional plane. He described to them how his actual shape in the third dimension would account for his changing size in their world.

Alas, the poor Flatlanders could not grasp what he was saying. They were stuck in their flat, two-dimensional perception. They could not see him as a sphere. They  could only see him as a circle that kept changing size. This frightened them. They thought they were witnessing a circle performing witchcraft. In their panic, they sought to destroy him.

Frustrated, the sphere finally gave up and left Flatland. The Flatlanders were simply unable to rise above their two-dimensional place to see a third dimension.

I want you to remember this story as you work through the five exercises. I want you to see yourself as the sphere, not as a Flatlander. I challenge you to open yourself up to new perceptions as you read your own mind. Don't close yourself to what you might discover. Don't be afraid to reframe your perceptions as you work through these exercises. Rise above Flatland!

Start with Self-Talk

Believing, perceiving, and choosing—these are the central themes that run through the various topics I've described to you. Using techniques for improving your memory as the gateway to knowing your mind, I talked about the power of beliefs, assumptions, and the I/You Concept, about creativity, about NLP, about perception, about listening, about intuition, and about choice, risk taking, and willpower.

Given all of this information, where do you start?

For me, the easiest place to start is *listening* to *myself*—listening to myself speak, observing myself as I react to situations and other people, and listening to my thoughts, my self-talk.

Throughout this book I have talked about self-talk. We are constantly engaged in self-talk. Whether we are listening to someone speak, listening to a radio, watching and listening to something on television, or just sitting and doing nothing, we are continuously talking to ourselves in our minds—we are engaged in self-talk all of our waking days.

So I suggest you start by examining your self-talk in several situations.

Pretend there's another person perched on your shoulder,  objectively observing you and listening to your self-talk when you are interacting with people. Let's give a name to that person. If you're a he, let's call him Patrick. If you're a she, let's call her Patricia. This will make it easier for me to describe the following exercises—whether you are a he or a she, I'll refer to the person perched on your shoulder as "Pat."

Now this is important. For the first three exercises, keep Pat on your shoulder, and keep a pencil and a notebook of some sort (like a diary) handy so you can record what Pat hears. You will revisit these notes later.

Exercise One: Study Yourself

This first exercise is designed to help you develop the habit of observing yourself when you interact with others, to read your own mind, to find out what's behind what you do and say. Psychologists refer to this as introspection. With all of the practice you've had from other exercises in the book, this should be an easy one for you.

For five days in a row, set Pat to work a few times each day, listening to your conversations and accompanying self-talk when you are interacting with someone. Keep your pad or diary handy so you can record exactly what Pat heard.

Pat needs to note the exact words you use, paying particular attention to the words that "color" your sentences, such as adjectives, adverbs, and qualifying phrases. Pat hearing you tell someone "That's an impossible task!" is very different from hearing you say, "That will be an easy task."

Pat also needs to note your tone of voice and observe what you are feeling as you talk.

Remember our discussion of the I/You Concept? Be alert for shifts to second person, particularly in situations that are uncertain, confusing, or even frightening.

Here's the hard part. Knowing Pat is listening, don't try to control your self-talk. Just keep Pat up there in the background, quietly listening and observing.

As soon after the conversation as is convenient, take a quiet moment by yourself to record what Pat heard and observed in your notebook and then reflect on it. Ask yourself questions like "Why did I choose *that* word?" and "Why was I experiencing *that* feeling?" and "Why did I react *that* way?"

Work at connecting your answers to those questions to beliefs you have and the assumptions you make—about yourself, about other people, and about the world in general. With Pat's help, study yourself just like a scientist would, with precision and objective discernment. If you find your choice of words or your reactions come from a self-critical or other negative place, don't berate yourself!

Practicing this technique several times each day for a few days will begin to turn it into a habit. You will soon find yourself automatically observing and listening to yourself and understanding more about yourself. Do this, and you will have taken the first step to reading your own mind.

Exercise Two: Challenge Yourself

This second exercise is designed to help you develop the habit of actively challenging yourself—challenging your core beliefs and assumptions. The main goal is not to change those beliefs and assumptions, unless you choose to do so. Instead, the main goal is for you to challenge them hard enough so you clearly understand the very foundations of your mind that drive you to make the choices you make.

Again, put Pat to work. Over the course of two weeks, expose yourself to as many situations as you can that you normally would not, and turn Pat loose to observe and listen to your reactions. In those situations, you may get caught up in your biases and judgments, but all the time, allow Pat to keep working. Keep Pat above it all, objectively listening and observing.

For example, suppose you are a dyed-in-the-wool Liberal, and you never watch Conservative talk shows. Challenge yourself. Take the time to sit down and watch a Conservative talk show with Pat perched on your shoulder, observing you and your self-talk.

Or suppose you are a dyed-in-the-wool Conservative, and you would never even consider reading that Liberal newspaper, the *New York Times*. Challenge yourself. Take the time to read several issues, particularly the editorials, again with Pat perched on your shoulder, observing you and your self-talk.

Perhaps you prefer more traditional music—soft ballads and easy listening.

Understanding and Reading Your Own Mind: All It Takes Is Practice

You find rap music offensive. Listen to some rap music—especially listen to the lyrics—again with Pat perched on your shoulder, observing you and your self-talk.

In other words, search for opportunities to expose yourself to situations in which messages are delivered that normally do not interest you, or you would not take the time to hear, or you would find offensive.

Again, take the time to record what Pat hears and observes. Examine what you record. Note your reactions—your self-talk, your feelings. Actively challenge the beliefs and assumptions on which they are based. Given Pat's information, you might find yourself changing some of them. Then again, you might not.

In either case, what you will end up with is a very clear understanding of your "mental models," the belief and assumption structures that determine what you think, what you say, and what you do, and ultimately, how you feel.

You will then have taken the second, very important step to reading your own mind.

Exercise Three: Expand Yourself

The first exercise in reading your mind was designed to help you begin making self-observation a habit. The second exercise helped you to challenge some of the foundations of your thinking. This third exercise is designed to help you take risks, to raise yourself above Flatland.

Identify three actions you have never chosen to take for one reason or another. Maybe you haven't done something because you will feel too embarrassed. Maybe you haven't done it because you are too afraid.

For example, perhaps you don't go out to your driveway in your bathrobe with your hair in curlers or uncombed to pick up

the morning newspaper because you will feel embarrassed if someone sees you. Or perhaps you avoid speaking in front of a group because you know you will be very anxious. Or maybe you take the stairs because you are afraid of elevators. In other words, list those actions you ordinarily choose not to do because of uncomfortable emotions such as embarrassment, frustration, or fear.

Of course, I'm not telling you to identify actions that truly could be life threatening, such as racing a car down the freeway at 130 miles per hour or hanging as far as you can off the top of a ten-story building. I'm talking about the more ordinary things you choose not to face in your daily life.

After you've identified the three actions, spend a few moments considering each. Visualize yourself taking the action. Imagine the emotions you experience as you do it. Then, think about the reasons you have used up until now for choosing not to do it. Finally, make a commitment to yourself you will take the action at the first opportunity.

Give yourself a week to take each action. And once more, put Pat to work, observing you and your self-talk as you actually do it.

Record Pat's information. Dig in and uncover the reasons why you are embarrassed or anxious or whatever has stopped you from taking the action in the past. Challenge your reasons. Are you embarrassed simply because you think people will disapprove of your action? Is that disapproval so important in your life that you will not act? Are you afraid because you think you will not do it well? Is that fear really rational, or does it just come from not having tried to master the action?

Determine if your reasons are really valid. If you suspect they are not, take a chance and try the action again. Keep at it again and again, until the reasons you had no longer make sense.

Completing this exercise brings you to a new level of reading your own mind, a level where you know it better than ever before—where you have a much-clearer perception of the reasons behind your choices and therefore your actions!

Exercise Four: Suspend Your Judgments

Completing the first three exercises should make this one easy. As you worked through them, you most probably noted various beliefs about yourself and how you behave. And, more importantly, you probably identified several situations that were ruled by your concern for how others see you.

Worrying about how people around you perceive you or think about you or make judgments about you makes it more difficult for you to access your intuition, which you will use in the next exercise. That kind of worrying comes from your automatic "shoulds" and "should nots"—those standards and judgments about yourself you may never have challenged or are even conscious of.

I should be smart. I should behave this or that way. I should dress a certain way. I wrote about all of this in chapter 10 when I explained how to cultivate your intuition.

I have found to truly know my own mind and tap into its deeper capabilities; I had to work hard at developing the ability to free myself from those judgmental strictures. I found I must keep an open mind, a willingness to look at my positions and situations from totally different perspectives, to allow myself to think outside of my perceptual box, to rise above Flatland.

So, here's the exercise.

Draw a line vertically down the middle of a piece of paper, dividing it into two columns. At the top of the first column, write the words "My Shoulds." At the top of the second column, write the words, "My Should Nots."

Now let your mind wander freely through the tangle of rules you make for yourself about the way you should and should not be in your daily life. List as many as you can in each column. After working through the first three exercises, it's very likely you have already identified several "shoulds" and "should nots." As you list each, leave a space below it, so you can write something there after your lists are complete.

When you think you have a reasonably complete list, sit back and spend a moment looking at it. Don't dwell on any one "should" or "should not" or try to challenge it. Simply note them all. Look at them as the structure that makes up your mental framework as you interact with the world.

Now consider each "should" or "should not," one at a time. Think about where it came from. Did you learn it early in life from one of your parents? A teacher? A minister? A book? More importantly, do you remember choosing it, or was it something imposed on you as the way things should or should not be. As you think about it, write down your observations in the space you made below it.

Then ask yourself some questions. "Is this something now, as an adult, I would freely choose on my own?" If yes, describe why you would choose it. And then ask yourself, "*Why* is it important? Is it really a fundamental principle I consciously choose to live by that does not restrict my ability to expand my mind? Or is it 'dictated' to me by something like a fear of what people will think? In other words, is it a 'should' or 'should not' I can choose to suspend because it restricts me?"

By the time you work your way through the entire list of your "shoulds" and "should nots," you will have a clearer picture of that part of your own mind that guides many of the choices you make every day.

Exercise Five: Use Your Subliminal Mind

By now, after having worked through the first four exercises, you have learned how to observe yourself and your self-talk. You have learned how to challenge and consciously choose your beliefs and assumptions. You have learned how to take risks and gain more active control of your life. You have learned how to suspend your judgments.

You now are in a position to practice the fifth exercise. As Emeril Lagasse of TV's Food Channel says, "*Bam!* Let's take it up a notch!"

This last exercise is directed at helping you use your intuition to fine-tune the reading of your own mind, to tap into levels most people do not usually reach.

In chapter 9, "Intuition: My Other Sense," I described a two-phase process for you to use to cultivate your intuitive ability. Remember the steps I described that my wife, Lois, and I use to cultivate our intuitive ability. If you followed and practiced those steps (pages 147–156), you are prepared for this exercise. If not, take the time to review chapter 9 before you continue reading this chapter.

Before I begin walking you through this exercise, I want to make several important points.

I gave you several tips in chapter 10, "Creativity: Expanding My Mind," for unleashing your creativity. Your flexibility to be creative is very much linked to your ability to tap into your intuition. The exercises you practiced to open up your creativity, to expand your mind outward, set up the opportunity for you to think outside the box. Now you are ready to use those new skills to—shall I say—expand your mind inward, to think deeper, inside the box, to levels of your own mind you can only tap with the conscious use of your intuition.

When I presented you with those creativity exercises and six outlandish conditions (pages 162–174) and questions to ask about them, I was helping you to stretch your mind, to open up your imagination to new possibilities.

In a moment I will ask you to use that same ability to stretch your mind and open up your imagination to tap into your intuition, to use the deeper part of your own mind.

The key to this exercise (I actually laid the groundwork for this in chapter 9) is being present in the moment, observing and capturing random thoughts and fleeting emotions, and assembling them into meaningful patterns. That's your intuition at work!

Here we go.

The easiest place to start this exercise is the one that feels the most familiar and natural to you. Gallup researchers introduce the notion of "talent," as a "four-lane highway in your head," something you enjoy doing and do so easily you just accept it as natural, like breathing. This "talent place" is the place in which you can most easily tap into your intuition.

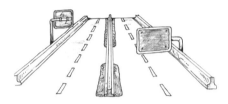

For some, it may be a natural mechanical talent to fix things, for others it might be a natural ability to organize and plan a task, for still others it might be a natural ability to interact with people.

Identify that place for yourself before you proceed.

Now think back to some recent instances where you utilized your talent.

Let's say, for example, you have a natural ability to organize and plan a task. Think about some recent instances in which you were doing so.

Now, pick one of those instances. Close your eyes, and in as much detail as you can remember, visualize yourself doing it. What did you do first? What were all of the elements and considerations involved? Then what did you do? And so on.

After you have thoroughly reviewed yourself doing it, you are ready to begin some mental brainstorming. Use a floating technique—let your mind slowly float through every moment of the incident, staying alert for feelings you experienced along the way that may have led you to choose one plan of action over another. Particularly note any random thoughts and fleeting emotions you experience as they bounce by. Don't examine or evaluate any of them—simply note them and allow your mind to work its own magic to assemble them into meaningful patterns.

Recall other times you utilized your special talent. For each situation, work your way through the steps of this fifth exercise.

Practice this for every example you can recall. After a while, you will suddenly find yourself aware of things that didn't strike you at the time—reasons for why you chose a particular action or inventive ways you could have done it differently.

You are putting an inner, deeper part of your mind to work for you. You are using your intuition.

When you've spent enough time in your talent place to feel comfortable with this floating technique, you are ready to use it in some other areas of your life.

Select an area of your life that is very important to you. It may be your relationship with your wife or your children or perhaps it's your career. At the top of a page, write down a word, such as "wife," that characterizes the life area you have chosen. Then, as rapidly as you can, free associate to that word—below it, write down the first word that comes to your mind. Then quickly write down below that word the next word that comes to your mind, and then the next, and so on.

When the associations slow down significantly (like the popping slows and stops when you're popping corn), put your pencil down, sit back, and examine your list of free associations.

Why did that particular word come to mind? What feelings are associated with it? How is it connected to the word before it and the word after it? My guess is you will discover some dimensions to that important part of your life that may not have been so clear before.

You've Been Reading Your Mind

By asking you to systematically work your way through the five exercises I've presented in this chapter, I've provided you with a pathway for reading your own mind. You've learned much more about yourself. You have challenged your beliefs and assumptions and are more aware of why you make the choices you make. You have taken risks to expand your experience. You have confronted your "shoulds" and "should nots" and have learned how to suspend your judgments. And you have used your intuition to access the deeper part of your mind. You truly have been reading your own mind.

As I personally have experienced and have emphasized many times in this book, I must be able to read my own mind before I can read the minds of others.

Having now cultivated the ability to read your own mind, you, too, are better prepared to read the minds of others.

CHAPTER FOURTEEN

At Last: Reading *Their* Minds

> The observation of others is colored by our inability to observe ourselves impartially. We can never be impartial about anything until we can be impartial about our own organism.
>
> —*A. R. Orage (1873-1934)*
> *Editor, author, essayist*

I'm sure you've been waiting for this chapter as you've been reading this book. The more faithfully you worked your way through the many exercises I presented to you along the way, the more prepared you are for the exercises in this chapter, designed to show you how to read the minds of others.

As you work your way through the exercises in this chapter, keep in mind what you've learned about yourself, particularly the challenges you made to your beliefs and assumptions—your mental filters. The more you are in touch with your own filters, the more effective you will be at reading the minds of others. As I stressed before and cannot stress enough, you must be able to read your own mind before you can read *their* minds.

In the previous chapter, I used Pat, perched on your shoulder, to help you listen and observe. In this chapter, I'm asking you to ask your friends to help you work through some of these exercises.

Also, in the last chapter, I used listening to self-talk as the starting point for learning how to read *your own* mind. I am again using listening to self-talk as part of the starting point in this chapter.

However, it becomes more complicated when I read the minds of others. Not only do I continue to listen to my self-talk and observe myself, I must, at the same time, listen to *their* words as they speak to me, to their choices of words, and to the way they deliver those words.

Exercise One: Study Them without Interacting

This first exercise is only a warm-up to reading the minds of others. You won't be able to verify the conclusions you draw about the people you are observing because you will be simply observing them and not interacting with them. The purpose of this warm-up is to help you train yourself to direct your attention to listening to and observing them and drawing hypotheses about them. Later on, you'll practice an exercise designed to help you determine how successful you are at reading their minds.

Having learned how to read your own mind, your task now is to turn your focus on observing others, to use the knowledge you have gained about yourself to figure out what's behind what they do and say.

The key word here is "focus," which means concentrating your attention on the other person. Yes, you will be thinking and reacting as you watch the person. But other than monitoring your thoughts and reactions to identify any filters that may be operating as you observe the person, you must make every effort to fully concentrate on paying attention to them.

Here's the task.

Pick out a TV talk show that comes on every day, like *Larry King Live* on CNN or a similar show, in which various people are interviewed talking about a variety of situations. The key is to find a daily show that involves different guests conversing about different topics.

For several days in a row, faithfully watch the program. Constantly listen to what people say and how they say it, and closely watch them. As you did with yourself in the last chapter, watch for the words that "color" their sentences—the adverbs, adjectives, and qualifying phrases that confer meanings to their sentences. Again, keep a pad of paper on hand to record your observations and conclusions.

As you listen to their words, listen to their tone of voice and watch their nonverbal behavior. Again, remember the I/You Concept. Be alert for a person shifting to second-person statements, particularly when he or she is describing disturbing or frightening moments.

Use what you learned when you reflected on your own self-talk. Make some inferences about their beliefs and assumptions that enable you to answer questions like "Why did they choose *that* word?" and "Why did they express *that* feeling?" and "Why did they react *that* way?"

Use your inferences about a particular person to speculate on the mental model driving his or her choices of words, tones of voice, and nonverbal behaviors. Determine if the mental model you come up with about that person holds up from one sentence to another, or from one segment of the program to another, if the person is on more than one segment.

Continue watching the program each day and recording your observations and conclusions until you reach a point where you are automatically doing it, without even consciously focusing on it as a task to do.

Again this exercise is a warm-up exercise. Your focus is primarily on the other person. The whole point is to help you develop the habit of listening to and observing people as they talk, without getting caught up in your own biases and judgments.

Exercise Two: Study Them While You Interact

Now you are prepared to do more than just observe another person. In this exercise, you interact with the other person, observing *both* of you at the same time. And here's where it becomes more complicated. It's not just your filters—it's *both* sets of filters operating at the same time.

I READ MINDS—AND SO DO YOU!

Remember the diagram on page 93 where I showed you how my beliefs and assumptions act as filters influencing what I hear, what I see, and what I do? Now two people are involved—myself and the other person. This adds another piece to the diagram, and it now looks like this:

Whew! Here's where the complication begins. To make it easy, let's say I'm interacting with my friend Bill.

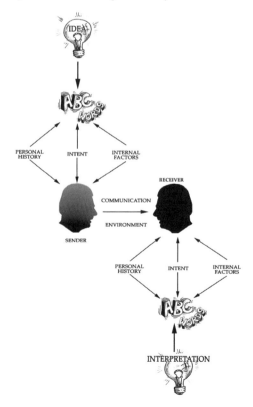

My message to Bill originates in my thoughts, with my intention to communicate something. I choose the words I think will convey the meaning I intend. Already what I'm about to say is being filtered through my beliefs and assumptions. I then deliver my message, saying what I set out to say, along with a host of nonverbal cues. While I'm saying it, even the environment we are in (the context) influences how it comes across, such as noises around us. Now Bill hears my words. To make sense of what he hears me saying, he interprets its meaning by filtering it through his beliefs and assumptions.

Because of all of these filters acting in each of us, the final understanding Bill has of my message may be different from the one I intended to send. It's amazing that we human beings can ever communicate anything effectively to one another!

So my challenge when I read Bill's mind while the two of us are interacting is to engage in two sets of actions at the very same time.

On one hand, I must analytically listen to my own self-talk and analytically observe myself in action.

On the other hand, I must analytically listen to what Bill says and analytically observe how Bill is saying it.

It is important for you to keep these two simultaneous sets of actions in mind as I describe the second exercise.

Carry out this exercise with four or five people you know, one at a time. And test your own success as you move from one person to the next, so you can learn to sharpen your skills.

For the first person you choose, try to pick a topic that is not too controversial. Start with a topic to talk about that is familiar to both of you. Maybe it's a movie you've both seen or a book you've both read or an event you both have attended. (As you move on to persons two, three, four, and five in this exercise, "up the ante"—move to topics that are increasingly more controversial.)

Start your interaction by asking their opinion about the topic, not by expressing your own opinion. For example, "What did you think of the movie?" or "What did you think about the book?"

As your friend responds, listen to your self-talk and observe your feelings. At the same time listen to what your friend says and observe the way he or she is saying it.

You already have some opinions of your own as you listen to your friend's answer. Take care! Work hard at not allowing your own opinions to filter what you hear as you listen to and observe your friend. The more you disagree with that person, the more important this becomes—actively guard against the temptation to immediately form counter responses to what you are hearing.

Again, be a scientist. Like you did in the first exercise, use what you are hearing and perceiving to formulate some hypotheses about the beliefs and assumptions underlying what your friend is communicating to you. As you come up with those hypotheses from time to time during your conversation, actively test them by asking your friend questions to see if you are right.

As I said earlier, continue practicing this exercise with several different friends, picking more controversial topics as you become more confident at what you are doing.

The reason I recommend more controversial topics as you proceed is to make sure you involve yourself in interactions that elicit emotional responses, as increasingly controversial topics tend to do.

I know from my experience that by the time you have diligently worked through this exercise with several friends, you will be amazed at how good you will become at it.

Exercise Three: Understand Their Point of View

When I read the minds of others, being accurate while listening to and observing them—getting past each of our filters—is not enough. I must also *understand* their point of view. That is the task involved in this third exercise.

I have a friend who was a college professor for many years. I remember his telling me a story about himself that is particularly appropriate here.

He told me that while he was in graduate school, he did not feel as smart as the rest of his fellow students. He was working as a graduate assistant in a lab with a half dozen other graduate students whom he perceived as very talented. One of them moved around the lab singing selections from various operas—something my friend had not been exposed to in the more rural culture in which he was raised. Another fellow student loved to work crossword puzzles. The only thing is, he would work crossword puzzles written in Latin! Still another fellow student continuously (and dramatically) walked around quoting passages from Shakespeare's plays.

All of these students appeared to my friend as more sophisticated, cultured, and educated than he was. As a result, in spite of the fact that he earned mostly *A*s in every course he took, my friend did not feel very smart. By the time he received his doctorate, even though he had taken many courses, he still didn't believe he knew very much.

But then he became an associate professor in a state university and started teaching what he had learned. Lo and behold! He very quickly discovered he knew far more than he thought he did!

He concluded that the act of describing to others what he had learned in graduate school solidified what he had learned. He realized communicating what he had learned to others was the final step in his learning process. By teaching his specialty to others, he achieved a deeper understanding of it.

I'm going to use my friend's story as a metaphor in this third exercise, which is designed to help you gain a true understanding of what another person is communicating to you as the two of you interact.

Again, interact with several friends, one at a time. Select friends who you know in advance have different opinions than you about various topics—philosophy, politics, religion, etc. During the course of this exercise, interact with as many friends as you need in order to feel confident that you have learned how to truly understand another person.

Let's say the first friend's name is Betty. Tell Betty you are practicing an exercise you have read about that will help you understand another person's point of view. Get her permission to interview her. Then, with a pencil and pad to record what you hear, interview Betty.

Select topics about which both of you have different opinions. Ask Betty to describe what she believes about the topic—what is her point of view? Use all of the tips you have learned while reading this book to listen carefully and objectively to her.

When you think you have enough information, tell Betty you want to use your notes to write a description of her point of view and you then would like to come back and have her read it to see if you understood her correctly.

Then, like writing a small essay, use your notes to write a description of her point of view. As you choose your words while you write, restrain yourself from flavoring it with any of your biases. Your task is to capture and articulate her point of view as accurately as you can.

When you have finished, give it to Betty and ask her to read it and tell you if it is accurate. If there are places where you "got it wrong," even slightly wrong, discuss it with her so you come to know why you got it wrong; which of your own filters got in the way?

Repeat this exercise with other friends until you feel confident you have mastered the art of understanding another person's point of view, even though you may disagree with their point of view.

I have found that the more I come to understand another person's point of view, the more accurately I am able to read his or her mind.

Exercise Four: Step into Their Shoes

This exercise takes the concept of understanding even further.

While learning the role of a character they are about to portray, some actors do everything they can to "get into the skin" of that character. Recently, for example, I saw actor Jim Carrey being interviewed about a movie he starred in called *The Man in the Moon*. This movie was about the life of the late Andy Kaufman who was a successful, but personally tormented, standup comic.

Jim Carrey described how he virtually became that character in his everyday life. He was Andy Kaufman with all of his friends and with everyone he met. He totally assumed the role.

Actors like Carrey know they can learn to truly understand the mind of another person by "being" that person, by stepping into his or her shoes.

This fourth exercise is designed to give you a taste of that experience, to help you become even better at reading another person's mind.

I'm modeling this exercise after a technique used by debating teams. People on a debate team are trained to debate either side of an issue. In a contest, they don't know which side they will be debating, so they have to be prepared to debate either.

Here's the exercise. It has two steps.

First, select a friend who has many opinions that are very similar to your opinions. (In most cases, that shouldn't be too hard to do because we tend to associate with like-minded people.)

Choose someone who has views similar to you on political issues or childrearing or the way you think about religion or some such matter. The point is to choose a friend who stands pretty much in the same shoes as you do in some important part of their life.

Let's assume you choose such a friend whose name is Jerry. Tell Jerry you have been reading this book and would like his help in working through this exercise. Select an issue you both agree on and tell him you would like to practice debating it with him by arguing the other side of the issue, the other point of view.

Schedule a time and place for the debate and then go off by yourself to do a little research to prepare your arguments. While you are preparing, try to become a person who holds that other point of view, just like an actor would do.

After you've prepared yourself, meet with Jerry and try your hardest to persuade him to your "new" point of view, tell him to do his best to counter every argument you make, and then do everything you can to overcome the counterarguments he makes.

The second step of this exercise is for you to spend some time with another friend who shares the very side of the issue you were debating. Let's say his name is Joe. Your challenge is to engage Joe in a conversation about the issue, asking him to describe the reasons why he believes the way he does. Listen to him without attempting to counter any of his opinions with your own. Listen instead to your self-talk and observe your feelings as he talks. The idea is to see how much your experience with Jerry has led you to have a better understanding of Joe's point of view.

Practice this same set of exercises with some other friends. Get as much experience at this as you can. Your goal is to reach a deeper level of understanding of another person. Mastering the skill of standing in someone else's shoes will widen your knowledge of how other people think and illuminate the kinds of filters that are triggered when you converse with one another.

This skill is invaluable to you in reading the minds of other people.

You're Now Reading the Minds of Others

In the last chapter, I presented you with five exercises as a pathway for reading your own mind. You learned more about yourself, challenged your beliefs and assumptions to reveal why you make the choices you make, expanded your experience by taking risks, confronted your "shoulds" and "should nots" to learn how to suspend your judgments, and used your intuition to access the deeper part of your mind.

In this chapter, building on what you learned about reading your own mind, I presented you with four more exercises designed to show you how to read the minds of others. You learned how to fully concentrate on focusing your attention to listening to and observing another person, how to formulate some hypotheses about the beliefs and assumptions underlying what that person is saying without being influenced by your own mental filters, and how to truly understand another person and his or her point of view.

My intent in offering you all of these exercises is to help you become consciously aware of the influence of both your mental filters and the mental filters of any person with whom you are interacting. Fully attaining that ability leads you to a capability of not only reading your own mind but also the capability of reading the minds of others so easily that one day you find yourself doing it without even thinking about it.

It is in those moments that I personally have experienced my intuition moving into high gear. During my interaction with the other person, I almost instantly, intuitively know where the other person is coming from and what he or she is thinking. I am truly reading that person's mind.

I am absolutely certain, with diligent practice, you, too, can reach this level in reading the minds of others!

CHAPTER FIFTEEN

A Work in Progress: I Will or I Will Not

> Willingness is essential in any initiation or in making any dream come true. "I can't" often means "I won't." You can change "I won't" to "I will" with willpower.
> —*Marcia Wieder*
> *Lecturer, author*

Throughout this book, I consciously chose to use the first person singular "I" instead of the second person "you" used by many other authors, especially authors of self-help books. I did this because I wanted you to fully own, in your personal first person, what you were learning as you read through the chapters.

As the author, I wanted to be certain that I am still on target with what I say; that I truly accept, own, and believe what I am articulating. I decided I could best convey this to you by having you read what I wrote using "I" statements.

I wanted you to continue to be empowered with the benefits derived by reading my information with first-person statements, rather than the usual second-person statements found in most books. I believe I have succeeded in doing that.

Have You and I Achieved What We Set Out to Do?

It is now time for you to ask yourself three all-important questions. "Have I met my initial commitment to read and understand all of the material in this book?" "Have I interacted with all of the exercises in this book?" "Have I diligently practiced what I have learned along the way?"

If you can answer *yes I have*, to all three of these questions then you are in a great position to succeed at reading minds.

I suppose I could easily continue on with additional concepts and examples for another few chapters. After all, there are so many more concepts and methods designed to improve and enhance your mind skills that have not been covered here. I believe that by practicing and accomplishing all I have included in this book, I have positioned you to consciously and accurately read your own mind as well as the minds of others.

As I stated at the start of this book and have reinforced throughout these pages, before you can begin to learn how to read the minds of others, you must first learn how to read your own mind. That is precisely what this book has been all about.

However, I fully realize that after reading this book, you, as well as the many people who have seen my performances and have heard my presentations, may have some questions. Questions like these:

"Hey, wait a minute, what about my being able to do what I saw Anton Zellmann do at the medical conference? I heard him tell people exactly what they were thinking. He told one woman she was thinking of the birth of her baby, and he even named the baby's name. How did he do that?"

Or a question like this one. "I saw Anton at a presentation where he correctly revealed that a doctor was thinking about an award he had won in college. How did he do that?"

And then you may even consider asking me, "How come I can't do what I saw you do even after I did every exercise in your book? I read every word. Come on, what's the trick?"

Understanding the Facts as I Perceive Them

The trick is to *understand the facts*.

It's a fact. After reading this book, you may never be able to duplicate exactly what I have demonstrated from the platform or stage. Keep in mind you are attempting to do something that your beliefs, which have developed from your lifelong programming, may make it seem impossible for you to accomplish.

It's a fact. Every habit you have incorporated into your thinking and actions has been supported by repetition over these many years. It takes a great deal of time to undo and modify those habits.

It's a fact. Your beliefs and assumptions play a huge role in what you see yourself as capable of doing. You now know modifying your thinking and actions can only seriously begin once you have made the commitment to shift your thinking. It can only begin when you are willing to change self-defeating self-talk which is based on beliefs and assumptions that no longer serve a good purpose in your life.

It's a fact. If you attempt something that you have not previously attempted, you must consciously choose to do so and then willfully act on that choice.

It's a fact. Your ability to communicate is only as good as the proficiency of your communication skills. After all, isn't that what mind reading really is, an important facet of communication?

It's a fact. Unless you are at the top of your game, your level of skill at speaking, listening, and observation limits you. You are doubly limited by your own perceptions of both space and time. On one hand you are wired to tune into only so many vibrations of light, of sound, of aroma, of flavor, and of physical sensation. Yet, on the other hand, and I believe this is a crucial point, you are inherently limited by what you *think* about what you see, hear, smell, taste, and touch.

It's a fact. You are limited by all of the personal filters that result in your choices, deductions, and conclusions. Although it is not a simple task to accurately read your own mind and the minds of others, you are now so much better equipped to succeed. By shifting your thinking and behaviors you know you will be rewarded with more beneficial results.

Those are the facts as I see them. Ultimately you must evaluate all of the thoughts and information discussed on these pages. It's all up to you. Either *you will* or *you will not* choose to comprehend, utilize, and master this work.

The Payoff

Of course, it would be easy to simply discount it all and go about your business as usual, to allow the specific dynamics of your level of consciousness and your particular perceptions and beliefs to continue to influence who you are and who you will become. That would be rather easy.

And I clearly understand there is a great likelihood many people will continue to enjoy excellent results in their lives with whatever their thinking process has been prior to or even without reading my book.

My premise has been and continues to be that the material about which I have written is not specifically designed to repair any mental or relationship challenges you may be currently experiencing. Rather, I designed it to add new ideas, concepts, and tools to your set of skills and to assist you to enhance those mind skills you already use.

The payoff is simple. If you choose to shift your current thinking a bit, incorporate these concepts and methods of enhancing your mind skills into your habit system, you will more consciously design your future on your own terms. You will be in a position to communicate with yourself and others in a manner that is bound to enrich your relationships in ways that are beneficial to all concerned.

What This All Means to Me

When I began writing this book I wrote the following statement on a piece of paper and set it aside:

> But even today, with all of these profound thoughts and concepts churning around in my mind, I still find myself battling against my passion for indulging myself in eating more than my body requires and all too often drinking alcohol until I am in a stupor. I am not getting nearly enough exercise, and my cholesterol level is just over two hundred.
>
> About the only positive action I am currently taking that is directed towards my experiencing good health is I'm still taking all of my medications, vitamins, and supplements every day. Also, I meet with a therapist three to four times a month. I am learning more about myself, and bit by bit, I'm learning how to deal with my compulsive-addictive personality.
>
> I do not admit any of this with any amount of pride, nor am I berating myself. It is simply my truth at this moment in time. Nevertheless, I am focused on winning this crucial struggle.

It is now three years since I wrote the previous three paragraphs. I recently picked up that same piece of paper, and after reading the words I wrote back then I knew my circumstances had clearly changed for the better. Mostly because of my conscious desire to live out many of the concepts I have written about in this book.

After reading what I had written I decided it would make good sense to describe my current situation as I conclude the final chapter of this book.

I have come a long way with curbing my passion for indulging myself with alcohol and food. I stopped drinking for about sixteen months, and although I have an occasional desire to go back to my old habit of binging whenever I feel lonely, I am more able to make the choice to not do so. I am currently losing weight and am doing much better with a consistent exercise plan. I see my therapist once a month to keep myself on track.

My health issues are in check. I have been free of cancer in my bladder for more than six years, and I continue to demonstrate better-than-good results when I have my cholesterol checked—usually in the 141 to 147 ranges with acceptable LDL and triglyceride numbers as well. What a true joy to report I no longer experience being out of breath when I simply bend over to tie my laces.

Mentally, I am alert, productive, and enthusiastic about life. My relationships with my family and friends are peaceful and growing healthier each day.

As for my occupation, well a few days after 9/11/01, I decided to slow down on any travel and to take a sabbatical. So for the past two and one half years I have taken the time to really focus on finishing this book, and to develop my relationships with my mother, my wife, and my children. I also am very much involved in my community and in the weekly activities of my local Rotary Club.

Having recently decided I wanted to mentor others to duplicate my career as an "edutainer," I have entered into a verbal agreement with several younger and talented performers to license my presentations along with my personal consultation. This will provide each of them with a jumpstart on their careers and at the same time provide me with a stream of income while I pursue whatever opportunities the publication of this book may bring to me.

I Thank All Who Have Encouraged Me

I believe I've accomplished explaining exactly what I meant when I stated in the first chapter that I am convinced we human beings are already reading minds. More importantly, I have detailed what I must do to enhance my innate ability to read my own mind and to consciously communicate mind to mind with others.

I wrote in the first chapter I was going to "offer you a collection of techniques for improving your memory as a catalyst for enhancing your mental skills." I used memory as a gateway to many mental concepts such as concentration, creativity, intuition, beliefs, judgments, and so on. I believe I have succeeded in delivering on that promise. You now know how to store and recall all sorts of information, lists, as well as people's names.

Overall, of all of the concepts, ideas, and thoughts I have expressed in the previous fourteen chapters, I feel my idea of the I/You Concept is the most valuable. I believe I am onto something here that has the potential to cause a dramatic shift in the thinking patterns of at least the English-speaking world. Although my research to date also indicates people from many different countries think and speak in the equivalent of second person rather than first person in their native languages and consequently are also unconsciously limiting their potential.

Wow, I just stopped to read the last paragraph, and I realize it sounds very lofty. But I guess you get the picture—I am really psyched about the I/You Concept. Let me ask you this question. Has not the reading of this book, written almost entirely with first-person "I" statements in place of the usual second-person "you" statements, provided you with more insight to the truth and clarity of those statements?

As I said, I strongly believe I am onto something special here. In fact, I am already beginning to organize my thoughts, ideas, and research into a form I can use to write my next book with a working title of—you guessed it—"The I/You Concept."

233

My intention is to elaborate on my premise that speaking, listening, and reading in "I" statements can provide huge benefits to self and can open up, with "greater clarity," a more peaceful and productive dialog as I communicate with others.

Besides, as I stated in the first chapter, one of the reasons I wrote this book was to help me to organize my own thoughts and to more clearly understand who I am and how I created the results I have manifested in my life.

I am grateful to all who encouraged me to gather the thoughts and concepts I have been speaking about to thousands of audiences, and to place it all into this book in what I hope is a cohesive and understandable writing style.

I must admit that writing, rewriting, reading, and rereading the thoughts I have expressed on these pages has helped me to make immense shifts from many self-defeating thinking processes, habits, and behaviors to more positive thoughts and actions that are empowering and rewarding to me and all of those for whom I care and whom I love.

My sincere and fervent wish is that the collective material in this book has helped accomplish something very much the same for you!

INDEX

A

ability, 2, 6, 11, 13-15, 46, 53, 71, 82, 90, 93-94, 104, 110, 121, 125, 128, 134, 137, 138, 139, 140, 145, 147, 151, 153, 156, 161, 166, 168, 177, 178, 180, 185, 211-212, 214, 228, 232

ability to focus and concentrate, 71, 128, 178

achieve, 2-3, 16, 82, 84, 177, 181, 184, 187, 195, 199

active listening, 125, 183

adult ego state and listening, 126

aerobic exercise, 50-52, 180

assumptions, 14, 81, 84-99, 109, 112, 117, 120, 135, 146-147, 150-152, 166-171, 181-185, 194, 196, 203, 205-207, 210, 213, 215, 217-220, 225, 229

auditory thinking, 57-58, 60-66, 68-69, 71-72, 80, 100, 106, 120, 181

aware, 11, 19, 20, 25, 34, 37, 40, 57, 58, 70, 81, 94, 95, 120, 134, 150, 153, 171, 178, 180, 181, 196, 202, 213, 225

B

Bandler, Richard, 38, 55, 56, 68, 70

beliefs, 13-14, 81-83, 93-96, 97, 99-100, 111, 117-118, 120, 130-131, 135, 147, 150, 170-171, 181-185, 187, 194, 196, 198, 203, 205-210, 213, 215, 217-220, 225, 229-230, 233

beliefs and my memory, 99, 126

beliefs and my self-talk, 81-82

believe, 3, 14, 27, 80, 81-82, 85, 96, 100, 111, 161, 181

brain, 1, 6-7, 11, 13-14, 18, 22, 42-50, 52, 55-57, 94-95, 138, 150, 157, 161, 175-176, 178-181, 185

brain and aerobic exercise, 50-51

brain and emotional state, 51-52

brain and food groups, 49, 50-51, 180, 196, 230

brain and memory, 46-48

brain and neurons, 43-46

brain and neurotransmitters, 45, 47-48, 50

brain and nutrition, 48-50

brain and stimulation, 52-53

brain and the limbic system, 46, 47, 48
brain hemispheres, 175-176, 185

──────── C ────────

cerbral cortex, 47-48, 175, 179, 180, 185
change, 21, 36-40, 55, 82-84, 154, 206, 229
choice, 2, 4, 24, 27, 57, 80-82, 85, 95-97, 99, 105, 128, 141, 145, 151-152, 154-155, 177-181, 185, 187, 190-191, 195-196, 198-199, 203, 205-206, 208, 210-213, 216-217, 219, 222, 225, 229-231
comfort, 36-37, 97-98, 128, 181, 198, 208
communication, 1, 11, 13, 17-25, 55, 58, 64, 68-69, 123-124, 128-131, 160, 175, 178, 219-221, 228, 230, 233-234
communication and internal factors, 18-23
communication and the environment, 17, 20-21
communication and the receiver, 21-23
communication and the sender, 18-20
communication demons, 23-25
communication intent, 18-23
communication process, 22-24
concentrate, 2, 4, 7, 71, 125-126, 128, 178, 183, 216, 225
confidence, 35, 69, 191
confident, 5, 10, 37, 41, 69, 149, 191, 220, 222
conscious, 4, 12-13, 16, 28, 33, 36, 97, 105-106, 121, 131, 136-138, 145-148, 151-153, 156, 159-160, 182, 184-185, 187, 192, 209-211, 217, 225, 228-230
corpus callosum, 175, 185
creative 1, 7, 14, 83, 161, 165-166, 169, 171-174, 176, 184, 191, 211
creative ability, 1, 14, 166, 168
creativity, 40, 83, 97, 161-176, 184, 185, 190, 193, 203, 211, 233
creativity and framing, 171-175
creativity and my assumptions, 166-171
creativity and my brain, 175-176
cultivating my intuition, 147-156

D

Dahlke, Arnie, 145-146, 202
defensive behavior, 19, 22, 39, 40
depression, 46, 51
developing my creative skill, 161-165

E

effective listening pyramid, 125-127, 134
emotional state, 51-52
  emotions, 7-8, 12, 46, 48, 51, 62, 65, 118, 154, 180, 208, 211-212, 22
exercises, self-test,
  A.I.R, 104-106
  beliefs and risk taking, 97-98
  concentration, 71, 120
  conscious intuition, 147-155, 184
  creativity, 162-165
  creativity and assumptions, 166-174
  listening, 123-124
  listening pyramid, 126-134
  NLP, 59-60, 67
  Optimist Creed, 29-31
  perception, 112-117
  picture association, names, 107-110
  read others mind, 216-224
  read own mind, 204-213
  remembering names, 100-104
  rhyming number pegs, 71-80
  testing assumptions, 87-93
experience, 2, 13, 15, 24, 27-28, 30-31, 34, 36, 40, 55-58, 62, 64-67, 104, 118, 121, 130, 132, 136, 143-147, 150-151, 153, 171-172, 178-181, 184-185, 187, 197-198, 205, 208, 212, 214, 223-225, 230
eye-accessing cues, 63-64

F

facial expressions, 1, 126, 127
filter, 22, 93, 94, 126, 130-131, 181, 215-220, 222, 224-225, 230
filter of my beliefs and assumptions, 93-95
first person speaking, 28, 31-33, 35, 37, 40-42, 177, 179, 227, 233
flatland, 201-203, 207, 209
framing, 52, 138, 171-173, 184, 203

G

Grinder, John, 55, 68, 70, 81

I

I/You concept, 13, 27-33, 35-36, 40, 97, 178, 203, 205, 217, 233
idea, 1, 18-19, 24, 79, 121, 132, 146, 148, 154, 161, 177, 183
imagination, 4, 6, 11, 28, 179, 184, 197, 211
influences on my perception, 118-119
information, 6-9, 11, 14, 19, 37, 43, 57, 62, 69, 72, 77-79, 95, 99, 105, 125, 128, 130, 137-138, 154-155, 175, 178, 183, 185, 199, 207-208, 222, 233
intuition, 3, 14, 40, 135-156, 159-161, 183-185, 201, 203, 209, 211-214, 225, 233
intuition: a real life example, 138-144
intuitive ability, 137, 147, 151, 153, 156,

J

judgments, 126, 130-131, 134, 146-147, 150-152, 184, 206, 209, 211, 214, 217, 225, 233

K

kinesthetic, 57-58, 60, 62, 65-72, 80, 100, 103-104, 107, 181, 182
kinesthetic memory, 65, 67
knowledge, 7, 9, 35, 43, 45, 58, 63, 69, 100, 118, 130, 136, 181, 216, 224

L

learning, 2, 6, 8, 25, 40, 43-45, 52, 56-59, 60, 66, 69-70, 101, 121, 137, 151, 161, 170, 177, 183, 196, 215, 221, 223, 227
listening, 7, 14, 17, 22-24, 29, 33-34, 68-69, 81, 93, 96, 105, 120, 123-135, 155, 179-180, 183-185, 191, 199, 203-206, 215-217, 219-220, 222, 225, 229, 234
listening and practice, 133-134

M

memory, 1-4, 6-7, 9, 11, 13-14, 16, 36, 41, 43, 45-48, 50, 52-53, 55-58, 65-67, 69-74, 76, 78, 79-82, 94-96, 100-101, 104, 119-

120, 135, 161, 163, 176-183, 185, 197, 203, 233
memory ability, 6, 46, 53, 82, 177-178, 18
memory and concentration, 71
memory and my brain, 46-48
memory and perception, 119-121
memory as a link to other skills, 3-6
mental abilities, 2, 6, 11, 55, 98, 177, 193
mental skills, 2, 3, 94, 177, 181, 184, 187, 200, 232
mentalist, 142, 143, 192
mind, 1-2, 4, 6-7, 9-16, 18, 25, 27-28, 43, 55-57, 62-63, 65, 67, 70-71, 75, 79, 80-81, 95-97, 105-106, 110, 119-121, 124, 126, 129, 133, 136-138, 140-142, 144-155, 160, 161-162, 169-170, 174-175, 177-179, 181-185, 187, 192, 194, 197-198, 200-204, 20-216, 219, 220, 222-223, 225, 228-230, 232
mind reading, 80-81, 227, 229
mind skills, 2, 12, 137, 192, 228, 230

——————— N ———————

NLP, 14, 55-56, 60, 64-66, 68, 70-71, 81, 100, 120, 129, 180, 185, 203

NLP and my memory, 65-80
nonverbal communication, 20-21, 129-130, 134, 183, 199, 217, 219

——————— O ———————

Optimist International's Creed, 29-30
Ornstein, Robert, 175

——————— P ———————

parental messages, 33-34
perception, 2, 7, 13-14, 21-23, 83, 85, 110, 111-113, 116-121, 135-137, 150, 155, 161, 170, 178, 183, 185, 187, 197-198, 203, 208, 229-230
perception and memory, 119-121
perceptual context, 112-118
perfect memory abilities, 6-8, 80
physical, 11, 13, 17, 24, 45-46, 51-52, 57, 62, 70, 130, 146, 149-150, 156, 228
Pierce, Penny, 150
pop the balloon, 104-107
positive thinking, 82
potential, 11, 43, 144, 233
power of my assumptions, 85-93
preferred patterns of thinking, 59-63

processes 11, 57, 58-61, 141, 175, 180-181, 185, 234
psychic, 1, 9-11, 13, 135, 137, 139-140, 142, 144, 178

───────── Q ─────────

Quotes, 1, 17, 27, 43, 55, 81, 111, 123, 135, 137, 161, 177, 187, 201, 215, 227

───────── R ─────────

reality, 12, 28, 85, 118, 137
reason, 83, 111, 137, 148, 151, 198, 208
recall, 2, 7, 48, 50, 63, 65, 71-72, 75-76, 109-110, 121, 159, 177-178, 181-182, 191, 196-197, 213, 233
reflect, 5, 142, 205, 217
reframing, 52, 98, 171-173, 184, 203
remember, 8-9, 11, 14, 44, 46-47, 49, 51-52, 62, 66, 69-72, 75, 78-80, 82, 94, 100-101, 104-106, 108, 110, 119-120, 125, 130, 133, 157, 178, 180-183, 199, 210, 212
responsibility, 144
rhyming number pegs, 71-80
risks, 40, 97-100, 181, 185, 203, 207, 211, 213, 225
Rotary, 156, 158, 192, 193-196, 199, 232

rote memory, 7-9, 178

───────── S ─────────

scripts, 3, 27, 34, 36, 177, 179, 198
second person, 29, 31-37, 41, 179, 201, 205, 217, 227, 233
self-confidence, 35
self-confident, 41
self-discovery, 3, 55, 81, 177
self-esteem, 4
self-fulfilling prophecy, 37, 82
self-talk, 27-28, 63, 70, 81-82, 84, 100, 105, 110, 124, 132, 146, 148, 152-153, 178-179, 181, 183-184, 203-208, 210, 215, 217, 219-220, 224, 229
soul, 2, 10
spinal cord, 46
steps for effective listening, 127-133
stress, 20, 45, 48, 51-52, 149, 180, 194
success, 16, 25, 36, 51, 55, 58, 68, 156, 177, 184, 197, 199, 216, 219

───────── T ─────────

testing assumptions, 87-92
thinking, 3, 7, 12-14, 22-23, 28, 34-37, 40, 43-44, 47, 52, 55-57, 59-61, 63, 65,

70, 80, 82, 84, 100, 125, 129, 135-136, 138-140, 144, 146-147, 152-154, 157-158, 161, 169-172, 175, 179-181, 184-185, 190, 194, 207, 216, 225, 229-230, 233-234
thinking and my memory, 65-70
thinking outside the box, 35-36, 147, 169, 171-172, 184
three kinds of thinking processes, 57-63
three-minute exercise, 100
truth, 1, 35, 86, 175, 231, 233

U

unconscious, 11-12, 40, 97, 137-138, 144, 153, 155, 178, 187, 192, 195, 233
understanding, 2, 8, 12, 15, 17, 45, 71, 125, 136, 175, 187, 200, 206-207, 219, 221-224, 228

V

verbal, 18, 65-70, 100, 181-182, 232
verbal memory, 65, 67, 70, 181
vicious belief cycle, 82-83, 162
visual, 57, 60-69, 71-72, 80, 100, 103, 120, 181-182
visual memory, 65, 67, 120
visual thinking, 60
visualization and memory, 119-121
vulnerability, 33-35, 37, 40, 179

W

willpower, 196, 203, 214, 227

Z

Zellmann, Anton, 27, 42, 141-144, 187-200, 228
Zellman, Lois, 12, 13, 35, 58, 139-141, 143-144, 147, 190, 195, 211

About the Author

ANTON JOSEF ZELLMANN (Perceptionist and Edutainer) has been hailed as a gifted speaker, an inventive motivator, and an amazing entertainer.

Originally from New York City, Zellmann spent his early years working in theatrical and entertainment circles. He later pursued a ten-year career as an award winning sales and marketing consultant.

During the past twenty-eight years Zellmann has delivered over ten-thousand presentations at trade shows, meetings, and motivational seminars, during which he instructs sales and management personnel and trade show attendees how to achieve more from the "business of life" by understanding and using the innate mental and intuitive powers he claims we all possess.

Zellmann claims that everyone is *"Reading Minds."* He suggests mind reading is not some uncanny or exclusive ability some people have and others do not.

He asserts with conviction, "You are reading my mind at this very moment! This thought I am expressing as you read this paragraph is emanating from my mind and being received into your mind. The same process takes place during conversation between two people or groups of people. Mind reading is simply another expression of communication. And yet this communication process is more complex than most people realize. In this book I reveal, through personal stories and hands-on exercises, how to understand and improve this extraordinary human interaction."

For information about engaging Anton Josef Zellmann as a speaker or to conduct a workshop call 1 800 347-9813, visit my website at www.zellman.com, or send an E-mail to anton@zellmannpublishing.com.